POP

Rebuking the Devil

United States Conference of Catholic Bishops
Washington, DC

Cover image: Getty Images.

First Printing, May 2019
Third Printing, August 2019

ISBN 978-1-60137-608-4

Contents

INTRODUCTION

Does the Devil Exist?

Make no mistake about it: there is a devil. He is alive and active in today's world and shows no signs of letting up. He presents a serious threat to our eternal destiny. He seeks the ruin of our souls.

Sometimes the devil makes his presence known in obvious ways, but most often he does so in a subtle, insidious manner. Rarely does he manifest himself in the frighteningly dramatic fashion often depicted in Hollywood films and in literature in the horror genre about demonic possession and evil spirits; most often, he attempts to sway us toward self-destruction by appealing to our appetites, our passions, and our inclinations for comfort, pleasure, and self-absorption.

Some currents of thought express doubt that the devil is a real entity. Spiritual beings often are dismissed as mere myths in our modern age. An analysis[1] by the Center

---

1 See a comprehensive CARA analysis of the 2011 University of Maryland study at: "A New Age Old Scratch?" on "1964 CARA Research Blog," Aug. 24, 2017. *http://nineteen-sixty-four.blogspot.com/2017/08/a-new-age-old-scratch.html.* Original 2011 study: "Faith and Global Policy Challenges Questionnaire," Sept. 9-19, 2011. Program on International Policy Attitudes (PIPA), University of Maryland School of Public Policy. *http://www.cissm.umd.edu/publications/faith-and-global-policy-challenges-questionnaire-0.*

for Applied Research in the Apostolate at Georgetown University (CARA) of a 2011 University of Maryland study found that although belief in the devil's existence has remained fairly level among American adults in recent decades, at about 70 percent, fewer and fewer believe he is a "living being." Just 31 percent of all adults and just 17 percent of Catholics thought the devil to be a "living being" rather than a "symbol of evil." While studies in recent decades have shown that US adults show belief in the devil's existence, at about 70 percent, a more recent 2011 study reveals that the quality of this belief among Catholics is now more oriented toward thinking of the devil as a symbol rather than as an actual personal entity. "The devil" or "Satan" is frequently regarded as nothing more than a handy metaphor for human weakness, or for the presence of evil in the world, or as a simplistic way of explaining it. At the same time, ironically, there appears to be an unhealthy interest in evil spirits and forces in our culture, as evidenced by a popular fascination with the occult and with exorcisms.

Yet, as Pope Francis has pointed out, the devil has been around seeking the corruption of human souls throughout all of history. As he said in 2013, "The devil is on the first page of the Bible and he is still there on the last, when God has his final victory" (Morning Meditation, Oct. 11, 2013).

The "first page of the Bible" refers, of course, to the creation narratives in the book of Genesis, where we first meet the devil in the Garden of Eden. There, appearing as a "cunning" serpent, the devil tempts our first parents into disobeying God's command, using what Pope Francis—who is given to clever turns of phrases and cultural references—has termed "snake-tactics" and "fake news." That original sin, passed on to all of humanity, "began the tragic history of human sin," the pope said (Message for World Communications Day 2018). Thus began the endless "spiritual battle" between good and evil that every human soul must face.

Yet immediately, God announced a remedy. In what the Church Fathers called the *protoevangelium*, or "first Gospel," God promises a Redeemer. Addressing the serpent, he states: "I will put enmity between you and the woman, / and between your offspring and hers; / He will strike at your head, / while you strike at his heel" (Gn 3:15, *Lectionary*). The serpent, the devil, will continue to attack and wound humanity, the offspring of the woman; but one of her "seed" will strike a fatal blow ("strike at your head") and defeat the serpent. Already, just as the devil succeeds in introducing sin into the world, God pledges to send a Savior who will triumph over sin and death.

Pope Francis's mention of the last page of the Bible points to Revelation, whose final chapters speak of how the devil "was thrown into the pool of fire and sulphur" to be "tormented day and night forever and ever" (Rv 20:10).

Earlier in Revelation is report of a "war in heaven" in which St. Michael and his angels defeat "the ancient serpent, who is called the Devil and Satan, who deceived the whole world," along with his angels, casting them down to earth

(Rv 12:7-9). This is a flashback, as it were, to Satan's rebellion against God that resulted in his expulsion from heaven, an event that predated the fall of humanity.

Between these books of Scripture, we find many other mentions of the devil, demons, and evil spirits. When it comes to proper names, he most often is called Satan ("accuser"), but also is named "Beelzebul, the prince of demons" (Mt 12:24; Lk 11:15; see Mk 3:22), Lucifer or "Morning Star" (see Is 14:12), or Beliar (2 Cor 6:15). He is called "the tempter," "the ancient serpent," "the evil one," "the accuser of our brothers," the one who "deceived the whole world," "the god of this age," "the dragon," and even "ruler of the power of the air" among other descriptive titles (1 Thes 3:5; Rev 20:2; Eph 6:16; Rev 12:10; Rev 12:9; 2 Cor 4:4; Rev 12; and Eph 2:2).

After Genesis, the devil gets his first extended mention in Job, where Satan puts the pious and affluent Job to the test by stripping him of his family, prosperity, and health. In Wisdom we find a significant passage to which Pope Francis occasionally alludes: "For God formed us to be imperishable, the image of his own nature he made us. But by the envy of the devil, death entered the world, and they who are allied with him experience it" (Wis 2:23-24). Elsewhere in the Old Testament we find references to demons, to evil spirits, and to Lucifer.

A New Testament passage that Pope Francis draws upon frequently in reflecting upon the devil's actions is the temptation of Jesus in the wilderness, where he notes how Christ responded to this assault: "Jesus gave us an example: never communicate with [the devil], you may not speak with this liar, with this fraud that seeks our damnation" (Morning Meditation, Chapel of the Domus Sanctae Marthae, Nov. 25, 2016) The parables of Christ that mention the devil and the various accounts of Jesus casting out demons also give the pope opportunities to reflect on the characteristics of the Evil One.

In his homilies and addresses, in his audiences and meditations, and in his interviews and his apostolic exhortations, Pope Francis addresses with regularity the topic of the devil and his works. As a Jesuit, his thought is heavily influenced by St. Ignatius of Loyola, founder of the Society of Jesus and author of the *Spiritual Exercises*. St. Ignatius taught extensively about the battle between good and evil, about how we must choose between the "two standards" of following Christ or following the ways of the devil, as well as about our need for sound discernment of spirits. Pope Francis offers practical pastoral guidance—culled from the wisdom of the Church—for resisting temptations and doing spiritual battle with the "evil one," the "ruler of the world" (Jn 14:30).

This book draws upon these various sources and presents, in his own words, a survey of Pope Francis's teachings on the devil.

CHAPTER I

The Devil, His Existence, and His Attributes

"I believe that the devil exists," wrote Cardinal Jorge Maria Bergoglio, the future Pope Francis, in his 2010 book *On Heaven and Earth,* and "his greatest achievement in these times has been to make us believe he doesn't exist."

The *Catechism of the Catholic Church* has a lot to say about the devil. It describes Satan as "the angel who opposes God," who with other rebellious angels "refused to serve God and his plan" and now "try to associate man in their revolt against God" (no. 414). Tempted by the devil, our first parents lost their trust in God and disobeyed God's command, thus allowing the devil "a certain domination" over humanity (no. 407). This original sin resulted in a loss of original holiness and justice; transmitted to all humanity, it wounded human nature, leaving it "weakened in its powers, subject to ignorance, suffering and the domination of death, and inclined to sin" (nos. 417-418).

Yet we know the story of the battle against Satan has a happy ending. "Victory over the 'prince of this world' was won once for all at the Hour when Jesus freely gave himself up to death to give us his life," states the *Catechism* (no. 2853). And again, "By his Passion, Christ delivered us from Satan and from sin. He merited for us the new life in the Holy Spirit. His grace restores what sin had damaged in us" (no. 1708).

The word "devil" derives from the Greek *diabolos* ("accuser" or "slanderer"), which in turn comes from *dia-ballein* ("to throw across"). The *Catechism* thus says the devil "is the one who 'throws himself across' God's plan and his work of salvation accomplished in Christ" (no. 2851)

It's an apt image: to disrupt God's will and draw human souls into disobedience and eternal separation from God is the devil's whole purpose on earth.

The devil is not a character to be taken lightly, Pope Francis has repeated in many and various ways.

"He is evil, he's not like mist. He's not a diffuse thing, he is a person," Pope Francis told the Italian Catholic channel TV2000 in a 2017 interview. "I'm convinced that one must never converse with Satan—if you do that, you'll be lost."

Satan "always pretends to be polite," and "that's how he enters your mind," the pope explained. "But it ends badly if you don't realize what is happening in time."

In this chapter we will explore what Pope Francis has said about the existence of the devil and some of the characteristics by which he is known.

The Devil Is Real

Pope Francis is unequivocal about this: the devil is real. He is not a myth, nor is he a metaphor for human weakness, misfortune, or evil. He is, in the pope's words, "a personal being who assails us," and he has made his presence and reality known throughout human history.

"This Malign Power"

We will not admit the existence of the devil if we insist on regarding life by empirical standards alone, without a supernatural understanding. It is precisely the conviction that this malign power is present in our midst that enables us to understand how evil can at times have so much destructive force.

True enough, the biblical authors had limited conceptual resources for expressing certain realities, and in Jesus' time epilepsy, for example, could easily be confused with demonic possession. Yet this should not lead us to an oversimplification that would conclude that all the cases related in the Gospel had to do with psychological disorders and hence that the devil does not exist or is not at work. He is present in the very first pages of the Scriptures, which end with God's victory over the devil.

Indeed, in leaving us the Our Father, Jesus wanted us to conclude by asking the Father to "deliver us from evil." That final word does not refer to evil in the abstract; a more exact translation would be "the evil one." It indicates a personal being who assails us. Jesus taught us to ask daily for deliverance from him, lest his power prevail over us.

Apostolic Exhortation, *Gaudete et Exsultate*,
(*On the Call to Holiness in Today's World*), no. 160

Neither a Myth Nor a Symbol

[W]e should not think of the devil as a myth, a representation, a symbol, a figure of speech or an idea. This mistake would lead us to let down our guard, to grow careless and end up more vulnerable. The devil does not need to possess us. He poisons us with the venom of hatred, desolation, envy and vice. When we let down our guard, he takes advantage of it to destroy our lives, our families and our communities. "Like a roaring lion, he prowls around, looking for someone to devour" (1 Pet 5:8).

Apostolic Exhortation, *Gaudete et Exsultate*,
(*On the Call to Holiness in Today's World*), no. 161

We Must Fight Against the Devil

The devil exists, and we have to fight against him. . . . If our faith is weak, the devil will defeat us.

Morning Meditation, Chapel of the Domus Sanctae Marthae, Oct. 30, 2014

The Devil Is Present in History

The second reading of the Mass presents a dramatic scene: a woman—an image of Mary and the Church—is being pursued by a Dragon—the devil—who wants to devour her child. But the scene is not one of death but of life, because God intervenes and saves the child (cf. Rev 12:13a, 15-16a). How many difficulties are present in the life of every individual, among our people, in our communities; yet as great as these may seem, God never allows us to be overwhelmed by them. In the face of those moments of discouragement we experience in life, in our efforts to evangelize or to embody our faith as parents within the family, I would like to say forcefully: Always know in your heart that God is by your side; he never abandons you! Let us never lose hope! Let us never allow it to die in our hearts!

The "dragon," evil, is present in our history, but it does not have the upper hand. The one with the upper hand is God, and God is our hope!

Homily, World Youth Day Mass,
Rio de Janeiro, Brazil, July 24, 2013

The Devil Has Existed Throughout History

Please, let's not do business with the devil. The devil is on the first page of the Bible and he is still there on the last, when God has his final victory.

Morning Meditation, Chapel of the
Domus Sanctae Marthae, Oct. 11, 2013

The Devil Exists Even Today

Watch out, the devil exists! The devil exists even in the 21st century. And we must not be naive. We must learn from the Gospel how to battle against him.

Morning Meditation, Chapel of the
Domus Sanctae Marthae, April 11, 2014

The Devil at Work in the World

In plain and general terms, the devil is evident all around us. Opposing God, he seeks to take advantage of the human condition and lead us to eternal death.

Evil in the Headlines

Look around us—it is enough to open a newspaper, as I said—we see the presence of evil, the Devil is acting.

General Audience, St. Peter's Square, June 12, 2013

"Terrible, Terrible Things in the World"

When you watch television, at home, remember these two things: there is a struggle against good and evil in the world, there are many suffering children, there are wars, there are dreadful things, because the struggle is between God and the devil. . . . There are terrible, terrible, terrible things in the world, and this is the devil's work against God; but there are holy things, saintly things, great things that are the work of God. There are hidden saints.

Address, Paul VI Audience Hall, Dec. 31, 2015

Evidence of the Evil One

We know that evil unfortunately is at work in our existence and around us, where there is violence, rejection of the other, closure, war, injustice. All of these are the work of the Evil One, of evil.

Angelus, St. Peter's Square, Feb. 18, 2018

"Struggle Between the Devil and God"

[I]n the world there is a struggle between good and evil—the philosophers say—a struggle between the devil and God. This still exists. When each one of us wants to do something cruel, that little bit of cruelty is an inspiration of the devil, who, through the weakness left within us by original sin, leads us to this.

Address, Dec. 31, 2015

The Devil Prowls "Like a Roaring Lion"

The devil does not need to possess us. He poisons us with the venom of hatred, desolation, envy and vice. When we let down our guard, he takes advantage of it to destroy our lives, our families and our communities. "Like a roaring lion, he prowls around, looking for someone to devour" (1 Pet 5:8).

Apostolic Exhortation, *Gaudete et Exsultate*, (*On the Call to Holiness in Today's World*), no. 161

"Manners of the Devil"

[I]t is God himself who abides among us to free us from self-interest, sin and corruption, from these manners of the devil: seeking success at all costs; seeking power to the detriment of the weak; having the desire for wealth; seeking pleasure at any price.

Angelus, St. Peter's Square, Dec. 4, 2016

Devil's Way "a Road That Leads to Death"

[The devil] could not endure that man be superior to him, that man and woman be made in the image and likeness of God. This is why he made war on them [and laid before them] a road that leads to death . . .

We all have to pass through death. Yet it is one thing to pass through this in the hands of the devil, and quite another to pass through it in the hands of God.

Morning Meditation, Chapel of the Domus Sanctae Marthae, Nov. 12, 2013

Hell Is Also Real

"Then he will say to those on his left, 'Depart from me, you accursed, into the eternal fire prepared for the devil and his angels," Christ tells us in his parable of the sheep and the goats (Mt 25:41). Hell exists because the devil exists, and it is a destination the demons have chosen for themselves. Satan would like also to make hell our destination, which is why he constantly tempts us, often in subtle ways, to distance ourselves from God by choosing evil over good. In the end, if we choose poorly, we risk condemning ourselves to hell, Pope Francis reminds us, which is the "road that leads to death" referenced above.

The Devil Chose Hell

There was a very proud angel, very proud, very intelligent, and he was envious of God. . . . He wanted God's place. And God wanted to forgive him, but [the proud angel] said, "I don't need your forgiveness. I am good enough!"

This is hell: It is telling God, "You take care of yourself, because I'll take care of myself." They don't send you to hell, you go there because you choose to be there. Hell is wanting to be distant from God because I do not want God's love. . . .

The devil is in hell because he wanted it. . . . [T]he devil [is] the only one we are sure is in hell.

Meeting, Parish of St. Mary, Mother of the Redeemer,
Tor Bella Monaca, Rome, March 8, 2015

First to Be Judged

The devil will be the first to be judged. There is an angel who will come and take the dragon, the ancient serpent, that is the devil Satan—clearly, as you can understand well with whom you are speaking—and will enchain [him] and throw [him] into the abyss. [There,] the devil, the ancient serpent, will be shackled so that he no longer might lure nations away, because he is the seducer.

Morning Meditation, Chapel of the
Domus Sanctae Marthae, Nov. 25, 2016

Hell Is Distancing Ourselves from God

Eternal damnation is not a house of torture; it is a description of the second death. It is a death. . . . Those who will not be received in the kingdom of God, because they did not approach the Lord: they are those who are always going down their own path, far away from the Lord, and passing by the Lord, moving away from him, alone.

Eternal damnation is the continual distancing of oneself from God, and it is the greatest suffering: that of an unsatisfied heart, a heart that was made to find God but, due to pride and overconfidence, became distanced from God.

Morning Meditation, Chapel of the
Domus Sanctae Marthae, Nov. 25, 2016

"Eternal Abyss"

The danger always remains that, by a constant refusal to open the doors of their hearts to Christ, who knocks on them in the poor, the proud, rich and powerful will end up condemning themselves and plunging into the eternal abyss of solitude, which is Hell.

Message for Lent 2016, Given Oct. 4, 2015

Enemy of God and Man

By his definitive rejection of God, Satan made himself God's enemy. As such, he opposes God and seeks to drive a wedge between God and man, which also makes the devil "the enemy of humanity."

Doesn't Want Us to Trust in God

[St. Therese of the Child Jesus] said that, at the end of her life, there was a struggle in her soul, and when she thought about the future, about what awaited her after death, in heaven, she felt as if a voice was saying: "But no, don't be foolish, darkness awaits you, only the darkness of nothing is awaiting you." . . . [That] was the devil who did not want her to trust in God.

Morning Meditation, Chapel of the
Domus Sanctae Marthae, Feb. 6, 2014

Opposes Evangelization

We must tell each other the truth: the work of evangelizing, of freely carrying grace ahead, is not easy, because we are not alone with Jesus Christ; there is also an adversary, an enemy who wants to keep men and women separate from God.

Address, Paul VI Audience Hall, June 17, 2013

Opposes Our Discipleship

The spirit of evil does not want us to become holy, it does not us to bear witness to Christ, it does not want us to be disciples of Christ. . . . The devil does not want us to become holy, he does not want us to follow Jesus.

Morning Meditation, Chapel of the Domus Sanctae Marthae, April 11, 2014

"Enemy of Humanity"

Where the Lord proclaims the Gospel of the Father's unconditional mercy to the poor, the outcast and the oppressed, is the very place we are called to take a stand, to "fight the good fight of the faith" (1 Tim 6:12). His battle is not against men and women, but against the devil (cf. Eph 6:12), the enemy of humanity.

Homily, Chrism Mass, Vatican Basilica, March 24, 2016

Hatred

Because he opposes God, and God is all love, the devil is steeped in hatred—hatred of God, hatred of God's will, hatred of those who love God and wish to remain obedient to him. Satan tempts us out of hate, says Pope Francis.

Hatred Is from the Devil

Understand this well: love is of God, then from whom does hatred come? Hatred does not come from God but from the devil! And the saints removed themselves from the devil; the saints are men and women who have joy in their hearts and they spread it to others. Never hate but serve others, the most needy; pray and live in joy. This is the way of holiness!

Homily, Solemnity of All Saints,
St. Peter's Square, Nov. 1, 2013

"Always a Troublemaker"

We also recognize in the Trinity the model for the Church, in which we are called to love each other as Jesus loved us. And love is the concrete sign that demonstrates faith in God the Father, Son and Holy Spirit. And love is the badge of the Christian, as Jesus told us: "By this all men will know that you are my disciples, if you have love for one another" (Jn 13:35). It's a contradiction to think of Christians who hate. It's a contradiction. And the devil always seeks this: to make us hate, because he's always a troublemaker; he doesn't know love; God is love!

Angelus, St. Peter's Square, June 15, 2014

Sown in Human Hearts

[Reflecting on those who martyred St. Stephen (Acts 7:54-60)]

It was not that they did not agree with what Stephen was preaching: they hated [Stephen, and] this hatred was sown in their hearts by the devil. It is the devil's hatred for Christ.

Morning Meditation, Chapel of the
Domus Sanctae Marthae, May 6, 2014

Seeks to Dehumanize

So many projects, except for one's own sins, but so many, many projects for the dehumanization of man are his works, simply because he hates man.

Morning Meditation, Chapel of the
Domus Sanctae Marthae, Sept. 29, 2014

Tempts out of Hate

Think how the prince of the world tried to trick Jesus in the desert. . . . [He] hates us. And what he did with Jesus, he will do with us.

Morning Meditation, Chapel of the
Domus Sanctae Marthae, May 4, 2013

The Tempter

Temptation is a universal experience. The tempter, the devil, is "everywhere," always seeking ways to exploit our weaknesses. Pope Francis has said the devil's "real victory" comes when he is able to "anaesthetize" our conscience and become its master.

"Lead Us Not into Temptation"

The one who leads us into temptation is Satan. That is Satan's craft. The meaning of our prayer is, "When Satan leads me into temptation, please God, give me a hand, give me your hand." It is like that painting in which Jesus holds his hand out to Peter, who is imploring him, "Lord, save me, I am drowning, give me your hand!" (cf. Mt 14:30)

Our Father: Reflections on the Lord's Prayer (Image, 2018), p. 94

We Know the Devil Through Temptation

In our lives, in the life of each one of us, we have many temptations. Many. The devil pushes us to be unfaithful to the Lord. Sometimes he pushes hard. . . . [T]he whole of the Lord's creation will be faced with this choice between God and evil, between God and the prince of this world.

Morning Meditation, Chapel of the
Domus Sanctae Marthae, Nov. 28, 2013

Even the Saints Are Tempted

[St. Pio of Pietrelcina (Padre Pio)] never denied his home town, he never denied his birth, he never denied his family. Indeed, in that time he lived in his home town for health reasons. That was not an easy time for him: his inner soul was sorely tormented and he feared to fall prey to sin, feeling he was being attacked by the devil. And this gives no respite, because he [the devil] is restless.

But do you believe that the devil exists? . . . You are not quite convinced? . . . Does the devil exist or not? *[The audience answers: "Yes!"]*. And he goes, he goes everywhere, he gets inside of us, he moves us, he torments us, he deceives us. And he [St. Pio] was afraid that the devil would attack him, would drive him to sin

Meeting, Visit to to San Giovannni Rotondo, 50th
Anniversary of the Death of St. (Padre) Pio, March 17, 2018

The Devil Is "Everywhere"

[O]ur weaknesses are everywhere, the devil is also everywhere, temptations are everywhere; but we must always try.

Address, Paul VI Audience Hall, Oct. 23, 2013

Numbs the Conscience

When the evil spirit is able to anaesthetize the conscience, we can say that this is his real victory: he becomes master of that conscience.

Morning Meditation, Chapel of the
Domus Sanctae Marthae, Oct. 9, 2015

Deceiver, "Father of Lies"

In order to tempt us, the devil uses tricks and deceptions. That is why Scripture—and Pope Francis—call him "the father of lies," among other descriptive terms. God is truth, and in opposing God, Satan embodies falsehood.

Liar

The devil is a liar, he is the father of liars.

Morning Meditation, Chapel of the
Domus Sanctae Marthae, Oct. 30, 2014

"Father of Lies"

We know where lies come from: in the Bible, Jesus calls the devil the "father of lies," a liar.

Morning Meditation, Chapel of the
Domus Sanctae Marthae, April 29, 2016

"Sower of Snares"

[S]nares are one of the strategies of the devil. He is a sower of snares. A seed of life, a seed of unity never falls from his hands—snares always snares: it is his method, to sow snares.

Homily, Chapel of the Governorate, Oct. 3, 2015

"Seductive Serpent"

We have heard this passage from the Book of Genesis, the first temptation: that of Adam and Eve. . . . The devil shows himself in the form of a seductive serpent and shrewdly seeks to deceive: he is an expert at this; he is the "father of lies," as Jesus calls him. [He] is a liar; he knows how to deceive; he knows how to cheat people.

Morning Meditation, Chapel of the
Domus Sanctae Marthae, Feb. 10, 2017

"He Defrauds You"

We think of Adam and Eve, how [the serpent] began by speaking with a sweet voice . . . [but] he is a liar; moreover he is the father of lies. He creates lies and is a fraud.[The devil] makes you believe that if you eat this apple, you will be like a god; he sells you something, you buy it, and in the end he defrauds you; he deceives you, and he ruins your life.

Morning Meditation, Chapel of the
Domus Sanctae Marthae, Nov. 25, 2016

"Father of Sin"

[The serpent] is the symbol of evil; it is the symbol of the devil: he was the most astute of all the animals in the earthly paradise. . . . The serpent is the father of sin, the one who caused humanity to sin.

Morning Meditation, Chapel of the
Domus Sanctae Marthae, April 4, 2017

Distractions

Often [the devil] hides his snares behind the appearance of sophistication, the allure of being "modern," "like everyone else." He distracts us with the view of ephemeral pleasures, superficial pastimes.

Homily, Mass in Rizal Park, Manila, Philippines, Jan. 18, 2015

"Con Artist"

Friends: the devil is a con artist. He makes promises after promise, but he never delivers. He'll never really do anything he says. He doesn't make good on his promises.

Address, "Costanera" Riverside Area,
Asuncion, Paraguay, July 12, 2015

Cheater and Swindler

The enemy always destroys: he makes you believe that this is the way and then, in the end, he leaves you on your own. Because remember this: the devil is a poor payer, he never pays well! He always cheats, he's a swindler!

Address, Paul VI Audience Hall , Aug. 7, 2015

Liar, Gossip, Divider

The devil is a liar and, what is more, he is a gossip, he loves going from one place to the other, seeking to divide, and he wants members of a community to speak badly of each other.

Homily, Midday Prayer, Shrine of the Lord of the Miracles, Lima, Peru, Jan. 21, 2018

Joyless Entertainer

The devil never gives you joy. He gives you a little entertainment, a "pantomime," makes you happy for a moment, but he never gives you that joy.

Address, Paul VI Audience Hall, Aug. 7, 2015

Numbs the Conscience

When the evil spirit is able to anaesthetize the conscience, we can say that this is his real victory: he becomes master of that conscience.

Morning Meditation, Chapel of the Domus Sanctae Marthae, Oct. 9, 2015

False Appearances

As part of his deception, the devil puts on airs, often presenting himself as courteous, intelligent, spiritually wise. He even appears sometimes, in St. Paul's words, disguised "as an angel of light" (2 Cor 11:14).

A Gentleman and Theologian

The Devil, tempting Jesus, boasts of good manners. Indeed, he presents himself as a gentleman, a knight in shining armor. He even presents himself as a theologian by quoting Holy Scripture. He appears to have everything right and neat on the outside, but his intent is always to lead others astray from the truth of God's love.

General Audience, St. Peter's Square, May 13, 2015

Intelligent

The devil is intelligent; he knows more theology than all the theologians together.

Morning Meditation, Chapel of the
Domus Sanctae Marthae, Sept. 26, 2014

Fake Spiritual Advisor

[The devil speaks] almost as though he were a spiritual master, as though he were an advisor.

Morning Meditation, Chapel of the
Domus Sanctae Marthae, April 11, 2014

"Very Polite"

[Sometimes] the evil one is hidden, he comes with his very polite friends, knocks on the door, asks permission, enters and lives with that man, in his daily life, and little by little gives him instructions.

Morning Meditation, Chapel of the
Domus Sanctae Marthae, Oct. 9, 2015

"Well-Mannered" Demon

What is worse: the recognizable demon that pushes you to sin so that you feel ashamed, or the well-mannered demon that lives within you and possesses you with the spirit of worldliness?

Via Twitter, @Pontifex, Oct 12, 2018

"Dressed Up as an Angel of Light"

It is true that the devil, and St. Paul says so, very often comes dressed up as an angel of light. He likes to imitate the light of Jesus. He makes himself seem good and speaks to us like that, calmly, just as Jesus spoke after fasting in the wilderness: work this miracle 'if you are the Son of God, throw yourself down' from the temple! Make a show of it! And he says so in a way that is calm.

Morning Meditation, Chapel of the Domus Sanctae Marthae, Sept. 3, 2013

Slyly Comes at Difficult Times

Ours is not a joy born of having many possessions, but from having encountered a Person: Jesus, in our midst; it is born from knowing that with him we are never alone, even at difficult moments, even when our life's journey comes up against problems and obstacles that seem insurmountable, and there are so many of them! And in this moment the enemy, the devil, comes, often disguised as an angel, and slyly speaks his word to us. Do not listen to him! Let us follow Jesus!

Homily, Palm Sunday, St. Peter's Square, March 24, 2013

Envious and Prideful

Two characteristics of the devil frequently addressed by Pope Francis are his envy and pride, two key attitudes that resulted in his rebellion and fall from grace.

"Came into the World Through Envy"

The Bible says that the devil came into the world through envy. A community, a family is destroyed by this envy that the devil teaches in the heart and causes one to speak ill of the other.

Morning Meditation, Chapel of the Domus Sanctae Marthae, Sept. 2, 2013

Envy of Humanity

Through the devil's envy, death entered the world . . . [The devil] could not endure that man be superior to him, that man and woman be made in the image and likeness of God. This is why he made war on them [and laid before them] a road that leads to death.

Morning Meditation, Chapel of the Domus Sanctae Marthae, Nov. 12, 2013

Pride Versus Humility

[*Quoting St. Augustine*] "It was pride that changed angels into devils; it is humility that makes men equal to angels."

Address, Paul VI Audience Hall, Dec. 22, 2011

No Room for Forgiveness

Only one was not forgiven, because he had so much pride he did not make way for forgiveness: the devil.

Morning Meditation, Chapel of the Domus Sanctae Marthae, Oct. 13, 2016

Shrewd and Cunning

The serpent was "the most cunning" of all the wild creature in the Garden of Eden (Gn 3:1), and this describes well the methods of Satan. It is a real danger to Christians that, as St. Paul expressed his concern for the faithful of Corinth, "as the serpent deceived Eve by his cunning, your thoughts may be corrupted from a sincere [and pure] commitment to Christ" (2 Cor 11:3). Pope Francis warns us always to be aware of this devilish attribute.

Saps Strength

The devil is cunning . . . and he will take away your strength.

Greeting, Vatican Basilica , March 12, 2015

"The Devil Is Shrewd"

The demon is shrewd: he is never cast out forever, this will only happen on the last day. . . . This is the devil's strategy: "You become a Christian, go forward in your faith, and I will leave you alone; I will leave you in peace. But then, once you have have grown accustomed to it, are no longer watchful and feel secure I will return." . . . St Peter said he is like a roaring lion prowling around us.

Morning Meditation, Chapel of the
Domus Sanctae Marthae, Oct. 11, 2013

"His Intention Is Destruction"

[Satan] is subtle: the first page of Genesis says so. He is subtle, he presents things as if they were good. But his intention is destruction.

Morning Meditation, Chapel of the
Domus Sanctae Marthae, Sept. 29, 2014

A Cunning Charmer

[The Book of Genesis] describes the serpent as "the most cunning" . . . He is a charmer that has the ability to fascinate, to charm you . . . He is a liar, he is jealous; it is because of the devil's envy—the serpent's envy—that sin entered the world.

Morning Meditation, Chapel of the
Domus Sanctae Marthae, Sept. 14, 2015

Sowing Evil in the Midst of Good

The parable [of the wheat and the weeds] has a twofold teaching. In the first place, it says that the evil in the world does not come from God, but from his enemy, the Fiend. It is curious, the Fiend goes out at night to sow the weeds, in darkness, in confusion; he goes where there is no light to sow the weeds. The enemy is astute. He has sown evil in the midst of good, so that it is impossible for us men to separate them properly; but God, in the end, will be able to do so.

Our Father: Reflections on the Lord's Prayer (Image, 2018), p. 106-107

Patient and Persistent

Although they sound like virtues, the devil's patience and persistence are part of his cunning and hate-filled nature: he is hell-bent, as it were, to win us over to the side of evil.

Cast Out, He Waits to Return

The evil spirit never tires. He was cast out, but patiently waits to return. When he returns he is pleased to find the house swept and put in order. Then he goes and brings seven other spirits, more evil than himself, and they enter and dwell there; and the last state of that man becomes worse than the first.

Morning Meditation, Chapel of the
Domus Sanctae Marthae, Oct. 9, 2015

"Doesn't Stay Still"

Struggle and battle are normal in life: the devil doesn't stay still and he wants his victory.

Morning Meditation, Chapel of the
Domus Sanctae Marthae, Jan. 31, 2014

Tireless Workers

The devil and his minions never sleep and, since their ears cannot bear to hear the word of God, they work tirelessly to silence that word and to distort it.

Homily, Chrism Mass, Vatican Basilica, April 2, 2015

The Divider

Satan is not a uniter, but a divider, Pope Francis constantly points out. He gives the devil yet another title, "the father of division." Envy is one of his weapons in this effort.

"Nettlesome"

We all know that the devil is "nettlesome," the one who always tries to divide persons, families, nations, and peoples.

Our Father: Reflections on the Lord's Prayer (Image, 2018), p. 105-106

Always Divides

The devil—we know—is the father of division, the one who always divides, always makes war, does so much evil.

Angelus, St. Peter's Square, Jan. 25, 2015

The Push of Sin

The devil came into the world through envy, the Bible says. It was the devil's envy that brought sin into the world . . . It is very much the strength of the devil, of sin, that pushes us to division, always!

Morning Meditation, Chapel of the Domus Sanctae Marthae, May 12, 2016

Division Through Envy

[Community] is so important because the devil seeks to divide us, always. He is the father of division; through envy he divides. Jesus enables us to see this path, that of peace among us, of love among us.

Morning Meditation , Chapel of the Domus Sanctae Marthae, April 29, 2014

"It Is His Job"

How many times have we heard that a person has a serpent's tongue, because he does what the serpent did with Adam and Eve, he destroyed the peace? [This] is an evil, this is an ill in our Church: sowing divisiveness, sowing hate, not sowing peace. . . . [T]he devil helps to do this because it is his work, it is his job to divide!

Morning Meditation, Chapel of the Domus Sanctae Marthae, Sept. 4, 2015

Accuser and Destroyer

Revelation refers to Satan as "the accuser of our brothers . . . who accuses them before our God day and night" (Rev 12:10). The devil accuses not to seek justice; instead, his goal is always "to destroy man," says Pope Francis.

"Great Accuser"

Who is the great accuser in the Bible? The devil! Either you act as Jesus, who forgives by giving his life, prayer, long hours there, seated, like those two [St. Leopold and St. Pio]; or you play the role of the devil who condemns, accuses.

Homily, Vatican Basilica, Altar of the Chair, Feb. 9, 2016

"Roams the Earth"

The "Great Accuser," as he himself says to God in the first chapter of the Book of Job, "roams the earth looking for someone to accuse."

Morning Meditation, Chapel of the
Domus Sanctae Marthae, Sept. Sept. 11, 2018

"Seduction to Destroy"

Satan always seeks to destroy man . . . from the beginning, the Bible tells us about this: Satan's seduction to destroy.

Morning Meditation, Chapel of the
Domus Sanctae Marthae, Sept. Sept. 29, 2014

Rapid Demolition of God's Work

The evil one is far more astute than we are, and he is able to demolish in a moment what it took us years of patience to build up.

Homily, Chrism Mass, Vatican Basilica, April 2, 2015

Going After the People of God

[Jesus Christ is] who [Satan and the demons] want to destroy; and when they cannot destroy Jesus the person, they seek to destroy his people; and when they cannot destroy the People of God, they make up humanistic explanations that actually go against man, against humanity and against God.

Morning Meditation, Chapel of the Domus Sanctae Marthae, Sept. Sept. 29, 2014

Loser

One thing we must never forget: it is Christ who will triumph over Satan in the end. In fact, Christ already has triumphed, the pope indicates.

Devil Is a "Loser"

God has defeated the devil, and he did it on the Cross. He defeated the devil, but in his own way. The devil is a loser and has been defeated. Do you know how dragons are? They have a very long tail, and even if they have been killed, they continue to shake that tail for a while. What happened to the devil is like what happens to big and scary dragons that are defeated and killed. Their long tail moves and can still cause damage. . . .

Jesus' death defeated death. The devil is a loser—don't forget it! He is like a dragon or a dangerous dinosaur that wags its tail for a while even if it's already dead.

"Dear Pope Francis: The Pope Answers Letters from Children Around the World," Loyola Press (2016), p. 23

"Prince of the World"

Jesus chose us and redeemed us, through the freely given gift of his love. With his death and Resurrection he redeemed us from the power of the world, from the power of the devil, from the power of the prince of this world.

Homily, Church of St. Bartholomew on Tiber Island, April 22, 2017

Victory Over the Serpent

Our victory is the cross of Jesus, victory over our enemy, the ancient serpent, the Great Accuser. . . .

Jesus was lifted up and Satan was destroyed. We must be attracted to the cross of Jesus: we must look at it because it gives us the strength to go forward. And the ancient serpent that was destroyed still barks, still threatens but, as the Fathers of the Church say, he is a chained dog: do not approach him and he will not bite you; but if you try to caress him because you attracted to him as if he were a puppy, prepare yourself, he will destroy you. . . .

The cross teaches us that in life there is failure and victory . . . [L]ook at it, it is our sign of defeat, it provokes persecutions, it destroys us; it is also our sign of victory because it is where God was victorious.

Morning Meditation, Chapel of the
Domus Sanctae Marthae, Sept. Sept. 14, 2018

Even the Devil Knows He Will Lose

In the Synagogue of Capernaum, there is a man who is possessed by an unclean spirit which manifests itself by shouting these words: "What have you to do with us Jesus of Nazareth? Have you come to destroy us? I know who you are, the Holy One of God." The devil tells the truth: Jesus came to destroy the devil, to ruin the demon, to defeat him. This unclean spirit knows the power of God and he also proclaims his holiness.

Angelus, St. Peter's Square, Jan. 28, 2018

CHAPTER II

How the Devil Acts in the World

There's an old Italian expression about the devil that Pope Francis has used on a couple of occasions: *"il diavolo fa le pentole, non i coperchi"* ("The devil makes pots, but not lids"). The sense of the proverb is this: the devil fills a pot and stirs it. Eventually the pot, lacking a lid, boils over, and its contents will be revealed to everyone. Evil may be difficult to discern at first, but before long it will be seen for what it is.

It's a message similar to that in the parable of the wheat and the weeds. Evil sometimes masquerades as good, but truth and justice will win out in the end.

The devil masquerades, too. As the great deceiver, the father of lies, he knows how to dress up something evil so that it appears as something good to vulnerable individuals. We need to be able to recognize the Evil One and how he manifests himself so that we can resist his influence.

The devil is known through his works and through his empty promises—his lies and deceptions. In the *Rite of Baptism* and in the *Renewal of Baptismal Promises*, the presiding priest or deacon asks: "Do you reject Satan? And all his works? And all his empty promises?" These questions relate to the devil's objective in the world, which is to lead souls into sin and thereby draw them away from God, away from their eternal home in heaven for which they were created.

His temptation of our first parents and their subsequent fall introduced sin into the human experience, and as a result all of humanity is marked with original sin and suffers its consequences: among these a wounded and weakened nature, an inclination toward sin, suffering, and physical death. "By our first parents' sin, the devil has acquired a certain domination over man, even though man remains free," says the *Catechism of the Catholic Church* (no. 407).

During his papacy, Pope Francis has often made reference to the temporal actions of the devil. He rightly correlates the devil's works with the presence of evil in the world—not only to war, persecution, and violence, but also to corruption in business, idolization of money, worldliness, and injustice. He speaks of how the devil foments divisions in marriages, families, communities, and even the Church itself; he notes how the enemy preys on our pride, sadness, bitterness, and despair, dispositions that make his false promises and temptations seem all the more enticing.

In the previous chapter we surveyed the Holy Father's insights into the devil's existence, identity, and general attributes. Here we present what Pope Francis has said about how the Evil One operates in his efforts to influence and destroy us.

The Temptation of Christ

From the story of Jesus' temptation by the devil in the wilderness (Mt 4:1-11; Lk 4:1-13), Pope Francis derives certain characteristics of the devil's strategy. Satan tried to divert Christ from accomplishing God's will, and he seeks to do the same to us.

Threefold Temptation: Riches, Vanity, Power

We think of the first time that this lord [the devil] appears in the Gospel; it is in a dialogue with Jesus. Jesus was praying and fasting for 40 days in the desert, and at the end he was rather tired and hungry. And [Satan] comes; he moves slowly as a serpent, and makes three proposals to Jesus: "If you are God, the Son of God, there are stones there, if you are hungry, turn them into bread"; "If you are the Son of God, why are you so tired? Come with me to the terrace of the Temple and throw yourself down, and people will see this miracle and without effort you will be recognized as the Son of God"; the devil tries to seduce Him and, in the end, as he had not succeeded in seducing Him, he makes the last proposal: "Let's speak clearly, I will give you all the power of the world, but you must adore me. Let's make a deal."

These are the three steps of the strategy of the ancient serpent, of the demon: first, to have things, in this case bread, riches, riches that lead one gradually to corruption, and this issue of corruption is not a fairy tale! It is everywhere. Corruption is everywhere: for two pence many people sell their soul, sell their happiness, sell their life, sell everything. That is the first step: money, riches. Then, when they have it, they feel important.

The second step: vanity. What the devil said to Jesus: "Let's go on the terrace of the Temple, throw yourself down, and make a great spectacle!"—to live for vanity.

The third step: power, pride, arrogance: "I will give you all the power of the world; you will be the one who commands."

This also always happens to us all in small things: we are too attached to riches, we are pleased when we are praised, like the peacock. And many people become ridiculous, so many people. Vanity makes one become ridiculous. Now, in the end, when one has power, one thinks one is God, and this is the great sin.

Homily, Chapel of the Governorate, Oct. 3, 2015

Wealth, Vanity, Pride

There are three temptations of Christ . . . three temptations for the Christian, which seek to destroy what we have been called to be; three temptations which try to corrode us and tear us down.

First, wealth: seizing hold of goods destined for all, and using them only for "my own people." That is, taking "bread" based on the toil of others, or even at the expense of their very lives. That wealth which tastes of pain, bitterness and suffering. That is the bread that a corrupt family or society gives its own children.

The second temptation, vanity: the pursuit of prestige based on continuous, relentless exclusion of those who "are not like me." The futile chasing of those five minutes of fame which do not forgive the "reputation" of others. "Making firewood from a felled tree" gradually gives way to the third temptation, the worst. It is that of pride, or rather, putting oneself on a higher level than one truly is on, feeling that one does not share the life of "mere mortals," and yet being one who prays every day: "I thank you Lord that you have not made me like those others . . ."

The three temptations of Christ. . . . Three temptations which the Christian is faced with daily. Three temptations which seek to corrode, destroy and extinguish the joy and freshness of the Gospel. Three temptations which lock us into a cycle of destruction and sin.

Homily, Area of the Study Center of Ecatepec, Feb. 14, 2016

"False Shortcut to Success and Glory"

Jesus is now ready to begin his mission; and as this mission has a declared enemy, namely, Satan, He confronts him straight away, "up close." The devil plays precisely on the title "Son of God" in order to deter Jesus from the fulfillment of his mission: "If you are the Son of God" (Mt 4:3, 6); and proposes that He perform miraculous acts—to be a "magician"—such as transforming stones into bread so as to satiate his hunger, and throwing himself down from the temple wall so as to be saved by the angels. These two temptations are followed by the third: to worship him, the devil, so as to have dominion over the world (cf. v. 9).

Through this three-fold temptation, Satan wants to divert Jesus from the way of obedience and humiliation—because he knows that in this way, on this path, evil will be conquered—and to lead Him down the false shortcut to success and glory.

Angelus, St. Peter's Square, March 5, 2017

Diversion from Humble Service

All three of the devil's temptations to Jesus were suggestions aimed at distancing Jesus from this path, from the path of service, from humility, from humiliation, from the act of love he made by his life.

Morning Meditation, Chapel of the Domus Sanctae Marthae, Jan. 7, 2014

The Temptation of Man

The devil tempts us insidiously with subtlety, seduction, even courtesy.

The Devil's Trap

What does the spirit of evil do to snatch us away from Jesus' path through temptation? The devil's temptations have three main characteristics, and we have to be aware of them in order to not to fall into his trap.

[T]he temptation begins subtly but then it grows and increasingly grows stronger. [Then] it infects someone else . . . it spreads to another and seeks to take root in the community. [Finally,] to calm the soul, it seeks to justify itself.

Morning Meditation, Chapel of the
Domus Sanctae Marthae, April 11, 2014

"Sometimes He Pushes Hard"

In our lives, in the life of each one of us, we have many temptations. Many. The devil pushes us to be unfaithful to the Lord. Sometimes he pushes hard. . . . [T]he whole of the

Lord's creation will be faced with this choice between God and evil, between God and the prince of this world.

Morning Meditation, Chapel of the Domus Sanctae Marthae, Nov. 28, 2013

"Demonic Fascination"

[W]e heard about another strategy, another way of waging war, Satan who seduces. He is a seducer; he is one that sows snares and is a seducer, and he seduces with fascination, with demonic fascination, leading one to believe everything. He sells skillfully with this fascination, he sells well, but in the end he pays poorly! It is his method.

Homily, Chapel of the Governorate, Oct. 3, 2015

Courteous Demons

[Reflecting on Jesus' parable of the unclean spirits, in which a demon is cast out of a man only to return with several others (Lk 11:15-26)]

[The demon] enters gently. He knocks at the door, asks permission to enter, rings the bell, returns politely . . .

This second time they are courteous demons, [and so] the man is unaware of it: they enter stealthily, they begin to be a part of the man's life, with their ideas and inspirations they even help the man to live better and they enter the man's life, enter his heart and they begin to change that man from within, but quietly, without making a racket. . . .

This way is different from forceful demonic possession; this is more of a "parlor" demonic possession, let's say. . . . It is what the devil does slowly in our lives in order to change the criteria, to lead us to worldliness: he camouflages himself in our manner of behavior and it is difficult for us to realize it.

Morning Meditation, Chapel of the
Domus Sanctae Marthae, Oct. 13, 2017

His Empty Promises

As the father of lies, the devil cannot be trusted. Yet, because he is so clever, he lures us in by presenting evil as good and promising us a happiness that ultimately he cannot deliver.

The "Snake-Tactics" of Disinformation

[P]reventing and identifying the way disinformation works also calls for a profound and careful process of discernment. We need to unmask what could be called the "snake-tactics" used by those who disguise themselves in order to strike at any time and place. This was the strategy employed by the "crafty serpent" in the Book of Genesis, who, at the dawn of humanity, created the first fake news (cf. Gn 3:1-15), which began the tragic history of human sin, beginning with the first fratricide (cf. Gn 4) and issuing in the countless other evils committed against God, neighbor, society and creation. The strategy of this skilled "Father of Lies" (Jn 8:44) is precisely mimicry, that sly and dangerous form of seduction that worms its way into the heart with false and alluring arguments.

In the account of the first sin, the tempter approaches the woman by pretending to be her friend, concerned only for her welfare, and begins by saying something only partly true: "Did God really say you were not to eat from any of the trees in the garden?" (Gn 3:1). In fact, God never told Adam not to eat from any tree, but only from the one tree: "Of the tree of the knowledge of good and evil you are not to eat" (Gn 2:17). The woman corrects the serpent, but lets herself be taken in by his provocation: "Of the fruit of the tree in the middle of the garden God said, "You must not eat it nor touch it, under pain of death" (Gn 3:2). Her answer is couched in legalistic and negative terms; after listening to the deceiver and letting herself be taken in by his version of the facts, the woman is misled. So she heeds his words of reassurance: "You will not die!" (Gn 3:4).

The tempter's "deconstruction" then takes on an appearance of truth: "God knows that on the day you eat it your eyes will be opened and you will be like gods, knowing good and evil" (Gn 3:5). God's paternal command, meant for their good, is discredited by the seductive enticement of the enemy: "The woman saw that the tree was good to eat and pleasing to the eye and desirable" (Gn 3:6). This biblical episode brings to light an essential element for our reflection: there is no such thing as harmless disinformation; on the contrary, trusting in falsehood can have dire consequences. Even a seemingly slight distortion of the truth can have dangerous effects.

Message for World Communications Day, Jan. 24, 2018

Recruiting with Lies

St. Ignatius has a famous meditation on the two standards. He describes the standard of the devil and then the standard of Christ. It would be like the football jerseys of two different teams. And he asks us which team we want to play for.

In this meditation, he has us imagine: What it would be like to belong to one or the other team. As if he was saying to us: "In this life, which team do you want to play for?" St. Ignatius says that the devil, in order to recruit players, promises that those who play on his side will receive riches, honor, glory and power. They will be famous. Everyone will worship them.

Then, Ignatius tells us the way Jesus plays. His game is not something fantastic. Jesus doesn't tell us that we will be stars, celebrities, in this life. Instead, he tells us that playing with him is about humility, love, service to others. Jesus does not lie to us; he takes us seriously.

In the Bible, the devil is called the father of lies. What he promises, or better, what he makes you think, is that, if you do certain things, you will be happy. And later, when you think about it, you realize that you weren't happy at all. That you were up against something which, far from giving you happiness, made you feel more empty, even sad.

Friends: the devil is a con artist. He makes promises after promise, but he never delivers. He'll never really do anything he says. He doesn't make good on his promises. He makes you want things which he can't give, whether you get them or not. He makes you put your hopes in things which will never make you happy. That's his game, his strategy. He talks a lot, he offers a lot, but he doesn't deliver.

He is a con artist because everything he promises us is divisive, it is about comparing ourselves to others, about stepping over them in order to get what we want. He is a con artist because he tells us that we have to abandon our friends, and never to stand by anyone. Everything is based on appearances. He makes you think that your worth depends on how much you possess.

Address, "Costanera" Riverside Area,
Asuncion, Paraguay, July 12, 2015

No Peace, No Happiness

[The devil] shows you things dressed up, and you believe that thing is good, that it will give you peace; you go there and in the end you don't find happiness.

Address, Paul VI Audience Hall, Aug. 7, 2015

Presents "Evil as Good, Falsehood as Truth"

False prophets can also be "charlatans," who offer easy and immediate solutions to suffering that soon prove utterly useless. How many young people are taken in by the panacea of drugs, of disposable relationships, of easy but dishonest gains! How many more are ensnared in a thoroughly "virtual" existence, in which relationships appear quick and straightforward, only to prove meaningless!

These swindlers, in peddling things that have no real value, rob people of all that is most precious: dignity, freedom and the ability to love. They appeal to our vanity, our trust in appearances, but in the end they only make fools of us. Nor should we be surprised. In order to confound the human heart, the devil, who is "a liar and the father of lies" (Jn 8:44), has always presented evil as good, falsehood as truth.

Message for Lent 2018

Opportunistic

The devil has a way of exploiting our vulnerabilities. Not only does he foster pride, greed, sadness, bitterness, and despair within us, he also uses these human inclinations to draw us into his web of deception and sin, thus preventing us from experiencing joy.

Sows Sadness, Mistrust

Wherever there are dreams, wherever there is joy, Jesus is always present. Always. But who is it that sows sadness, that sows mistrust, envy, evil desires? What is his name? The devil. The devil always sows sadness, because he doesn't want us to be happy; he doesn't want us to dream.

Wherever there is joy, Jesus is always present. Because Jesus is joy, and he wants to help us to feel that joy every day of our lives.

Address, Our Lady, Queen of Angels School,
Harlem, New York, Sept. 25, 2015

Plays on Our Discouragement and Sadness

I wish to say to you: joy! Do not be men and women of sadness: a Christian can never be sad! Never give way to discouragement! Ours is not a joy born of having many possessions, but from having encountered a Person: Jesus, in our midst; it is born from knowing that with him we are never alone, even at difficult moments, even when our life's journey comes up against problems and obstacles that seem insurmountable, and there are so many of them! And in this moment the enemy, the devil, comes, often disguised as an angel, and slyly speaks his word to us.

Homily, Palm Sunday Mass,
St. Peter's Square, March 24, 2013

Robs Us of Joy

St. Ignatius customarily represents the devil as a thief. He says that the devil acts as a captain who attacks our weakest points in order to win and take from us what he wants (*Spiritual Exercises*, 327). In our case, today, I believe he is looking to rob us of joy—as if he wants to rob us of the present moment—and of hope—of going out, of walking—which are the graces for which I ask most, and for which I ask for prayer for the Church in this time.

Address, Basilica of St. John Lateran, March 2, 2017

Makes Us Feel Worthless

Never think that you have nothing to offer or that nobody cares about you. Many people need you; think this.

Each of you think in your heart: "Many people need me." The thought, "No one needs me," as [Saint] Alberto Hurtado used to like to say, "is the voice of the devil." "No one needs me." The devil wants to make you feel you are worthless . . . and to keep things the way they are. That's why he makes you feel worthless, so that no one changes, because the only one that can make changes in society is the young person, each of you.

Address, Santiago, Chile, Jan. 17, 2018

Fosters Fear of Failure, Commitment

There is one particular puddle which can be frightening to young people who want to grow in their friendship with Christ. It is the fear of failing in our commitment to love, and above all, failing in that great and lofty ideal which is Christian marriage. You may be afraid of failing to be a good wife and mother, failing to be a good husband and father. If you are looking at that puddle, you may even see your weaknesses and fears reflected back to you. Please, don't give in to them! Sometimes these fears come from the devil who does not want you to be happy.

Address, Kampala, Uganda, Nov. 28, 2015

Inspires Pessimism in Evangelizers

We must tell each other the truth: the work of evangelizing, of freely carrying grace ahead, is not easy, because we are not alone with Jesus Christ; there is also an adversary, an enemy who wants to keep men and women separate from God and for this reason instills in hearts disappointment when we do not see our apostolic commitment immediately rewarded.

Every day the Devil scatters in our hearts seeds of pessimism and gall, and it is discouraging, we become discouraged. "It's no good! We've done this, that and the other and it's no good! And look how that religion attracts people whereas we don't!" It is the Devil who inspires this . . . [he] does not want us to be evangelizers.

Address, Paul VI Audience Hall, June 17, 2013

Manifests as Excessive Pride

When one feels one is a sinner, one feels worthless, or, as I've heard some—many—say: "Father, I am like dirt," so then, this is the moment to go to the Father. Instead, when one feels righteous—"I always did the right thing…"—equally, the Father comes to seek us, because this attitude of feeling "right" is the wrong attitude: it is pride! It comes from the devil. The Father waits for those who recognize they are sinners and goes in search of the ones who feel "righteous." This is our Father!

Angelus, St. Peter's Square, March 6, 2016

Foments Bitterness, Despair

[Reflecting on Jesus' threefold question to Peter, "Do you love me?" (Jn 21:15-19)]

Just as it did Peter, Jesus' insistent and heartfelt question can leave us pained and more aware of the weakness of our freedom, threatened as it is by thousands of interior and exterior forms of conditioning that all too often give rise to bewilderment, frustration, and even disbelief.

These are not of course the sentiments and attitudes that the Lord wants to inspire; rather, the Enemy, the Devil, takes advantage of them to isolate us in bitterness, complaint and despair.

Reflection at Profession of Faith,
Vatican Basilica, May 23, 2013

Money, Prosperity, and Corruption

Corruption comes in many forms, and it often is said that "power corrupts." But money—"the dung of the devil"—is often at its root. The pope warns that the devil "enters through the pocketbook" and can lead us toward corruption—not only in our personal lives, but in the business world and even within the Church itself.

"The Worst Social Evil"

Corruption is the worst social evil. It is the lie of seeking profit for oneself or one's own group with only the appearance of serving society. It is the destruction of the social fabric behind the semblance of fulfilling the law. It is the law of the jungle disguised by apparent social rationality. It is the deceit and exploitation of the weakest or least informed. It is the most vulgar selfishness, hidden behind apparent generosity.

Corruption is generated by the adoration of money and returns to the corrupt, a prisoner of that same adoration. Corruption is a fraud against democracy and it opens the doors to other terrible evils such as drugs, prostitution and human trafficking, slavery, organ trafficking, arms trafficking, and so on. Corruption is becoming followers of the devil, the father of falsehood.

Address, Sala Regia, Nov. 17, 2016

"Trap of Hyper-Efficiency"

The Church is neither a political movement nor a well-organized structure. That is not what she is. We are not an NGO, and when the Church becomes an NGO she loses her salt, she has no savor, she is only an empty organization

We need cunning here, because the devil deceives us and we risk falling into the trap of hyper-efficiency.

Preaching Jesus is one thing; attaining goals, being efficient is another. No, efficiency is a different value. Basically the value of the Church is living by the Gospel and witnessing to our faith. The Church is the salt of the earth, she is the light of the world. She is called to make present in society the leaven of the Kingdom of God and she does this primarily with her witness, the witness of brotherly love, of solidarity and of sharing with others. When you hear people saying that solidarity is not a value but a "primary attitude" to be got rid of . . . this will not do! They are thinking of an efficiency that is purely worldly.

Address, St. Peter's Square, May 18, 2013

False Security

Corruption is an easier sin for all of us who have certain power, be it ecclesiastical, religious, economic or political power. . . . The devil makes us feel secure: "I can do it."

I would like to stress only this: There is a moment when the tendency to sin or a moment when our situation is really secure and we seem to be blessed; we have a lot of power, money, I don't know, a lot of "things." . . . Sin stops being sin and becomes corruption. The Lord always forgives. But one of the worst things about corruption is that a corrupt person doesn't need to ask forgiveness, he doesn't feel the need.

Morning Meditation, Chapel of the
Domus Sanctae Marthae, Jan. 29, 2016

When Capital Becomes an Idol

An unfettered pursuit of money rules. This is the "dung of the devil." The service of the common good is left behind. Once capital becomes an idol and guides people's decisions, once greed for money presides over the entire socioeconomic system, it ruins society, it condemns and enslaves men and women, it destroys human fraternity, it sets people against one another and, as we clearly see, it even puts at risk our common home, sister and mother earth.

Address, Santa Cruz de la Sierra, Bolivia, July 9, 2015

Affluence and Exclusion of the Poor

Paul had to rebuke the Corinthians in his First Letter (11:17), while the Apostle James was even more severe and explicit (2:1-7): he had to rebuke these affluent communities, affluent Churches for affluent people. They were not excluding the poor, but the way they were living made the poor reluctant to enter, they did not feel at home. This is the temptation of prosperity . . . The devil must not be allowed to sow these weeds, this temptation to remove the poor from very prophetic structure of the Church and to make you become an affluent Church for the affluent, a Church of the well-to do—perhaps not to the point of developing a "theology of prosperity"—but a Church of mediocrity.

Address, Meeting with the Bishops of Korea,
Seoul, South Korea, Aug. 14, 2014

Love of Riches Compromises Our Dignity

[T]he possibility exists that this dignity, conferred on us by God, can be degraded . . . This happens when we negotiate our dignity, when we embrace idolatry, when we make a place in our heart for the experience of idols.

During the exodus from Egypt, when the people were tired because Moses delayed in coming down from the mountain, they were tempted by the devil and made an idol for themselves (cf. Ex 32). And the idol was gold. All idols have something of gold! This makes us think of the attractive force of riches, of the fact that man loses his dignity when riches take God's place in his heart.

Address, Clementine Hall, Sept. 15, 2016

How Money Destroys and Condemns

It is not easy to speak about money. It was said by Basil of Caesarea, a Church Father of the fourth century, and then taken up by St Francis of Assisi, that "money is the devil's dung"! Now the Pope also repeats it: "Money is the devil's dung"! When money becomes an idol, it commands the choices of man. And then it destroys man and condemns him.

Address, Paul VI Audience Hall, Feb. 28, 2015

"The Devil Enters Through the Pocketbook"

You know, greed does us so much harm: the desire to have more, more and more money. When we see that everything revolves around money—the economic system revolves around money and not around the person, around man, around woman, but around money—so much is sacrificed and war is made to protect the money. And because of this, many people don't want peace. There is more profit with war! Money is earned, but lives are lost, culture is lost, education is lost, so many things are lost. This is why they don't want it.

An elderly priest that I met years ago used to say this: the devil enters through the pocketbook, through greed. This is why they don't want peace!

Address, Paul VI Audience Hall, May 11, 2015

Worldliness

As children of God, we are in the world but not of the world; our treasure is in heaven. The devil attracts us to things of the world so as to confuse our identity and distract us from our true eternal destiny.

Worldliness Enslaves Us

Do we live as children or as slaves? Do we live as people baptized in Christ, anointed by the Spirit, delivered and free? Or do we live according to the corrupt, worldly logic, doing what the devil makes us believe is in our interests? In our existential journey there is always a tendency to resist liberation; we are afraid of freedom and, paradoxically and somewhat unwittingly, we prefer slavery.

Freedom frightens us because it causes us to confront time and to face our responsibility to live it well. Instead, slavery reduces time to a "moment" and thus we feel more secure, that is, it makes us live moments disconnected from their past and from our future. In other words, slavery impedes us from truly and fully living the present, because it empties it of the past and closes it to the future, to eternity.

Homily, Vatican Basilica, Dec. 31, 2014

We Are Children of God, Not of the World

God chose and blessed us for a purpose: to be holy and blameless in his sight (Eph 1:4). He chose us, each of us to be witnesses of his truth and his justice in this world. He created the world as a beautiful garden and asked us to care for it. But through sin, man has disfigured that natural beauty;

through sin, man has also destroyed the unity and beauty of our human family, creating social structures which perpetuate poverty, ignorance and corruption.

Sometimes, when we see the troubles, difficulties and wrongs all around us, we are tempted to give up. It seems that the promises of the Gospel do not apply; they are unreal. But the Bible tells us that the great threat to God's plan for us is, and always has been, the lie. The devil is the father of lies. Often he hides his snares behind the appearance of sophistication, the allure of being "modern," "like everyone else." He distracts us with the view of ephemeral pleasures, superficial pastimes.

And so we squander our God-given gifts by tinkering with gadgets; we squander our money on gambling and drink; we turn in on ourselves. We forget to remain focused on the things that really matter. We forget to remain, at heart, children of God. That is sin: forget, at heart, that we are children of God. For children, as the Lord tells us, have their own wisdom, which is not the wisdom of the world.

Homily, Mass at Rizal Park, Manila, Philippines, Jan. 18, 2015

Worldliness and Hypocrisy

[This] is an everyday temptation of Christians, ours, of all of us who are the Church: the temptation not of power, of the Spirit's power, but the temptation of worldly power. . . . [O]ne falls into that religious warmth which leads you to worldliness [and] that attitude which Jesus called hypocrisy.

Morning Meditation, Chapel of the Domus Sanctae Marthae, April 20, 2015

Coming Down from the Cross

[Reflecting on the crucifixion narrative in the Gospel of Luke (23:33-43)]

There is a second group, which includes various individuals: the leaders of the people, the soldiers and a criminal. They all mock Jesus. They provoke him in the same way: "Save yourself!" (Lk 23:35, 37, 39). This temptation is worse than that of the people. They tempt Jesus, just as the devil did at the beginning of the Gospel (cf. Lk 4:1-13), to give up reigning as God wills, and instead to reign according to the world's ways: to come down from the cross and destroy his enemies! . . .

[H]ow many times, even among ourselves, do we seek out the comforts and certainties offered by the world. How many times are we tempted to come down from the Cross. The lure of power and success seem an easy, quick way to spread the Gospel; we soon forget how the Kingdom of God works.

Homily, Solemnity of Christ, King of the Universe, St. Peter's Square, Nov. 20, 2016

A Shift of Values

When the demon enters so gently, politely, and takes possession of our attitudes, our values shift from service to God towards worldliness.

Morning Meditation, Chapel of the
Domus Sanctae Marthae, Oct. 13, 2017

Creator of Divisions

The devil is not a unifier, but a divider. He divides marriages, families, communities, and even the Body of Christ, his Church.

Distrust Between Man and Woman

[Reflecting upon the creation account in Genesis (2:18-24)]

This was how man was, he lacked something to reach his fullness; reciprocity was lacking.

Woman is not a replica of man; she comes directly from the creative act of God. The image of the "rib" in no way expresses inferiority or subordination, but, on the contrary, that man and woman are of the same substance and are complementary and that they also have this reciprocity. And the fact that—also in that parable—God molds woman while man sleeps means precisely that she is in no way man's creation, but God's. He also suggests another point: in order to find woman—and we could say to find love in woman—man first must dream of her and then find her.

God's faith in man and in woman, those to whom he entrusted the earth, is generous, direct and full. He trusts them. But then the devil introduces suspicion into their minds, disbelief, distrust, and finally, disobedience to the commandment that protected them. They fall into that delirium of omnipotence that pollutes everything and destroys harmony. We too feel it inside of us, all of us, frequently.

Sin generates distrust and division between man and woman. Their relationship will be undermined by a thousand forms of abuse and subjugation, misleading seduction and humiliating ignorance, even the most dramatic and violent kind. And history bears the scar. Let us think, for example, of those negative excesses of patriarchal cultures. Think of the many forms of male dominance whereby the woman was considered second class. Think of the exploitation and the commercialization of the female body in the current media culture. And let us also think of the recent epidemic of distrust, skepticism, and even hostility that is spreading in our culture—in particular an understandable distrust from women—on the part of a covenant between man and woman that is capable, at the same time, of refining the intimacy of communion and of guarding the dignity of difference.

General Audience, St. Peter's Square, April 22, 2015

Attacks Families and Married Couples

Families are the domestic Church, where Jesus grows; he grows in the love of spouses, he grows in the lives of children. That is why the enemy so often attacks the family. The devil does not want the family; he tries to destroy it, to make sure that there is no love there.

Married couples are sinners, like us all, but they want to go forward in faith, in fruitfulness, in their children and their children's faith. May the Lord bless families and strengthen them in this time of crisis when the devil is seeking to destroy them.

Address, Olympic Stadium, Rome, June 1, 2014

Destroys Families Over Small Matters

It's sad in a family when siblings don't speak to each other for a small matter; because the devil takes a small matter and makes a world of it. Then hostilities go on, often times for many years, and that family is destroyed. Parents suffer because their children don't speak to each other, or one son's wife doesn't speak to the other, and thus, with jealousy, envy. . . . The devil sows this.

Homily, San Michele Arcangelo a Petralata Parish, Rome, Feb. 8, 2015

Division Within the Church

In a Christian community, division is one of the gravest sins, because it makes it a sign not of God's work, but of the devil's work, who is by definition the one who separates, who destroys relationships, who insinuates prejudice. . . . Division in a Christian community, whether in a school, a parish, or an association, it is a very grave sin, because it is the work of the Devil.

General Audience, St. Peter's Square , Aug. 27, 2014

Division in Communities

Perhaps the most powerful message that you can offer to those around you, is this faith that reaches out in solidarity. The devil wants you to quarrel among yourselves, because in this way he divides you, he defeats you, and he robs you of faith.

Address, Chapel of San Juan Bautista, Asunción, Paraguay, July 12, 2015

"Takes Advantage of Everything"

Forgive and sustain each other because community life is not easy. The devil takes advantage of everything in order to divide us! He says: "I do not want to speak ill but . . ." and then the division begins. No, this is not good because it does not do anything but bring division.

Address, Assisi, Italy, Oct. 4, 2013

Sower of Discord

Jesus prays to the Father so that his [followers] may "become perfectly one" (Jn 17:23): he wants them to be "one" (v. 22), as He and the Father are. It is his last request before the Passion, and his most heartfelt: that there be communion in the Church. Communion is essential.

The enemy of God and man, the devil, cannot compete with the Gospel, with the humble power of prayer and of the Sacraments, but can do much harm to the Church by tempting our human weakness. The devil provokes arrogance, the judgement of others, closure and division. He himself is "the divider" and often starts off by making us believe that we are good, perhaps better than others: thus the ground is ready for the sowing of discord. It is the temptation of all communities and it can instill itself even in the most beautiful charisms of the Church.

Address, Paul VI Audience Hall, March 18, 2016

Divisive Even in Defending What Is Good

[Saint] Francis saw his brethren divided under the very banner of poverty. The devil makes us quarrel among ourselves, defending even the most holy things "with an evil spirit."

Meditation, Basilica of St. Mary Major, June 2, 2016

Division Through Heresy

John the Apostle is clear: "He who says that the Word did not become flesh, is not from God! He is from the devil." He is not ours, he is the enemy! Because first there was heresy—let's say the word among us—and this is what the Apostle condemns: that the Word did not become flesh. No! The incarnation of the Word is at the foundation: it is Jesus Christ! God and man, Son of God and Son of man, true God and true man.

Address, Visit with the Evangelical Pastor Giovanni Traettino, Pentecostal Church of Reconciliation, Caserta, Italy, July 28, 2014

Destruction, Like a War

The devil sows jealousy, ambition and ideas, but only to divide! Or he sows greed . . . [S]ince the early times there have been divisions, and division causes destruction in the Church: divisions destroy, like a war: after a war everything is destroyed and the devil goes away pleased.

Morning Meditation, Chapel of the
Domus Sanctae Marthae, Sept. Sept. 12, 2016

"The Father of Division"

"I belong to Paul"; "I belong to Apollo"; "I belong to Peter." . . . And thus they begin, from the first moment division begins in the Church. And it isn't the Holy Spirit who creates division! He makes something which seems rather like it, but not division. It isn't the Lord Jesus who creates division! He who creates division is actually the envious one, the king of envy, the father of envy: that sower of weeds, Satan. He barges in on the community and creates division, always. From the first moment, from the first moment of Christianity, there has been this temptation in the Christian community. "I am this; "I am that"; "No! I am the Church, you are the sect." . . . And thus who acquires us is he, the father of division.

Address, Caserta, Italy, July 28, 2014

Gossip and Speech

One of the major catalysts for division, says Pope Francis, is gossip, a theme to which he returns frequently. Along with the sins of speech we can include calumny and hypocrisy. The devil uses gossip to create mistrust and destroy relationships.

The Devil's Weapon

Gossip divides communities, it destroys communities. It is the devil's weapon.

Morning Meditation, Chapel of the Domus Sanctae Marthae, Jan. 23, 2014

Calumny and Defamation

Once you have sown the seeds of calumny or gossip, defamation, you have destroyed. The devil is cunning: he uses this, which is one of our weaknesses. He is cunning.

Address, Consistory Hall, Feb. 10, 2018

Gossiper as "Terrorist"

Divisions are a handy weapon that the devil uses to destroy the Church from within. He has two weapons, but the main one is division; the other is money. The devil enters through the pocket and he destroys with the tongue, with divisive gossip; and the habit of gossiping is a ploy of "terrorism." The gossiper is a "terrorist" who drops the bomb—gossip—in order to destroy.

Address, Clementine Hall, Sept. 9, 2016

"One Always Gossips in the Dark"

Gossip in a community hinders forgiveness and also leads to being more distant from one another, to distancing oneself from the others. I like to say that gossip is not only a sin—because to gossip is a sin, and go to confession if you do this. . . . It is a sin! But gossip is also terrorism! Because someone who gossips "drops a bomb" on the reputation of the other and destroys the other, who cannot defend himself or herself, because one always gossips in the dark, not in the light. And darkness is the kingdom of the devil.

Address, Paul VI Audience Hall, Sept. 17, 2015

Dividing the Clergy

[W]hat is the greatest enemy of these two relationships [between bishop and priests]? Gossip. Many times I think—because I too have this urge to gossip, we have it inside us, the devil knows that this seed bears fruit and he sows it well . . .

Meeting with Clergy, Palatine Chapel in the Royal Palace of Caserta, Caserta, Italy, July 26, 2014

Dividing Religious Communities

The devil is a liar and, what is more, he is a gossip; he loves going from one place to the other, seeking to divide, and he wants members of a community to speak badly of each other.

I have said this many times, and will repeat it here: Do you know what a gossiping nun is like? She is a terrorist, worse than those of Ayacucho [Peruvian city where terrorist assaults took place in 1982] years ago, worse, because gossip is like a bomb. The terrorist just like the devil goes in whispering and murmuring, throws the bomb, destroys and calmly walks off. No to terrorist nuns, no to gossip.

Homily, Shrine of the Lord of the Miracles, Lima, Peru, Jan. 21, 2018

Hypocrite as "Killer"

The hypocrite is capable of killing a community. He speaks sweetly, while judging a person harshly. The hypocrite is a killer. . . . [Hypocrisy uses] the same language as the devil who sows that duplicitous language in communities in order to destroy them.

Morning Meditation, Chapel of the
Domus Sanctae Marthae, June 6, 2017

Resistance

There is a temptation, Pope Francis says, for leaders in the Church to believe they are indispensable, or for the faithful to resist legitimate reform. The devil is sometimes behind theses tendencies.

Resistance to Reform

In this process, it is normal, and indeed healthy, to encounter difficulties, which in the case of the reform *[of the Church]*, might present themselves as different types of resistance. There can be cases of open resistance, often born of goodwill and sincere dialogue, and cases of hidden resistance, born of fearful or hardened hearts content with the empty rhetoric of "spiritual window-dressing" typical of those who say they are ready for change, yet want everything to remain as it was before.

There are also cases of malicious resistance, which spring up in misguided minds and come to the fore when the devil inspires ill intentions (often cloaked in sheep's clothing). This last kind of resistance hides behind words of self-justification and, often, accusation; it takes refuge in traditions, appearances, formalities, in the familiar, or else in a desire to make everything personal, failing to distinguish between the act, the actor, and the action (Cf. Homily, Domus Sanctae Marthae, Dec. 1, 2016).

Christmas Greetings to the Roman Curia,
Clementine Hall, Dec. 22, 2016

It Is the Devil Who "Petrifies"

Thus the charism is not preserved in a bottle of distilled water! Faithfulness to the charism does not mean "to petrify it"—the devil is the one who "petrifies," do not forget!

Address, St. Peter's Square, March 7, 2015

"Indispensable" Leaders

Dear brothers and sisters, there is great temptation for the leaders—I repeat, I prefer the term servants, those who serve—and this temptation for the servants comes from the devil, the temptation to believe they are indispensable, no matter what the task is. The devil leads them to believe they are the ones in command, who are at the center and thus, step by step, they slip into authoritarianism, into personalism, and do not let the renewed communities live in the Spirit. This temptation is such as to make "eternal" the position of those who consider themselves irreplaceable, a position that always has some form of power or dominance over others. This is clear to us: the only irreplaceable one in the Church is the Holy Spirit, and Jesus is the only Lord. . . .

It is appropriate that every service in the Church have an expiry date; there are no lifelong leaders in the Church. This happens in some countries where there is dictatorship. "Learn from me, for I am meek and humble of heart," says Jesus. This temptation, which is from the devil, makes one go from servant to master, one dominates that community, that group.

This temptation also makes one slide into vanity. . . . Power leads to vanity! And then one feels one can do anything, and then one slides into business dealings, because the devil always enters through the wallet: this is the devil's way in.

Address, St. Peter's Square, July 3, 2015

Persecution and Injustice

The devil, "the spirit of the world," hates: he hates humanity and, in particular, Christians, and so he spreads hatred, war, and persecution around the world.

Creator of War

God is the God of peace, there is no god of war: what creates war is evil, it is the devil, who wants to kill everyone.

Morning Meditation, Chapel of the
Domus Sanctae Marthae, Sept. 20, 2016

"Because the Spirit of the World Hates"

So many Christian communities are persecuted around the globe. More so now than in the early times. . . . Why? Because the spirit of the world hates. Persecution usually comes after a long road.

Morning Meditation, Chapel of the
Domus Sanctae Marthae, May 4, 2013

Martyrdom Results from Hatred

[Reflecting on the stoning martyrdom of Stephen (Acts 7:54-60)]

It was not that they did not agree with what Stephen was preaching: they hated [Stephen, and] this hatred was sown in their hearts by the devil. It is the devil's hatred for Christ.

In martyrdom we clearly see the battle between God and the devil. We see it in this hatred. . . . He stirred up hatred in the hearts of those people against Stephen, to persecute him, to revile him, and to utter all kinds of evil against him.

At Stephen's death, a persecution against everyone broke out. . . . [The persecutors] felt that they were strong: the devil aroused them to begin this great persecution.

Morning Meditation, Chapel of the Domus Sanctae Marthae, May 6, 2014

"Ecumenism of Blood"

God makes no distinctions between those who suffer. I have often called this the ecumenism of blood. All our communities suffer indiscriminately as a result of injustice and the blind hatred unleashed by the devil.

Address, Bangui, Central African Republic, Nov. 29, 2015

"Hatred of the Worldly Spirit"

The origin of hatred is this: since we are saved by Jesus, and the prince of the world does not want this, he hates us and causes persecution, which, since the time of Jesus and of the nascent Church, continues to our day.

How many Christian communities today are the object of persecution! Why? Because of the hatred of the worldly spirit.

Homily, Church of St. Bartholomew on Tiber Island, April 22, 2017

CHAPTER III

Our Defense Against the Devil

Christian discipleship constitutes a spiritual battle. If we wish to follow Christ, the devil will challenge us. It's a conflict we cannot escape. The stakes could not be higher, for our very souls are at stake.

"The way of perfection passes by way of the Cross," says the *Catechism*. "There is no holiness without renunciation and spiritual battle" (no. 2015).

Satan, that "ancient serpent," is the architect of all the obstacles to our heavenly destiny. But our faith tells us the battle is winnable, for the Church offers us the weapons we need to conquer temptation.

"For, although we are in the flesh, we do not battle according to the flesh, for the weapons of our battle are not of flesh but are enormously powerful, capable of destroying fortresses" (2 Cor 10:3-4).

Indeed, we know how the story ends, for we are assured that Christ has won the ultimate victory over sin and death, and therefore over Satan. All we have to do is keep our eyes on Christ and follow him in his victory march.

That's "all we have to do"—and yet Satan, that expert at deception, can lead us astray if we are not vigilant, Pope Francis tells us. Perseverance is required. Discernment is required. Fidelity to truth is required. And the grace of God is required.

Christ and Satan compete for our attention and allegiance. Yet our options do not always appear to us in stark black-and-white terms. We need careful discernment to distinguish good from evil. We have fundamental choices to make.

Pope Francis once recalled a question the prophet asked of the people: "How long will you go limping on two feet?" The pope described this image as "not standing firm with either God nor with idols, having one foot in one place and the other foot in another." He related it to another expression: "This person is well with God and with the devil" (Meditation, *Domus Sanctae Marthae*, June 10, 2016).

Pope Francis is clear: we cannot be well with both God and Satan. In another meditation he stresses that we cannot "do it by halves"—we cannot both worship God and "play games with the prince of the world" (Meditation, Nov 28, 2013). We must be all in with Christ.

Here we examine the pope's frequent exhortations on the spiritual battle we all face: the weapons and techniques we have at our disposal to defend ourselves from the devil's assault, and how the Church provides support and guidance in that struggle to "reject Satan, and all his works, and all his empty promises."

The Battle Between God and the Devil

"Put on the armor of God so that you may be able to stand firm against the tactics of the devil," says the Letter to the Ephesians (6:11). "For our struggle is not with flesh and blood but with the principalities, with the powers, with the world rulers of this present darkness, with the evil spirits in the heavens" (6:12). Scripture, the Church fathers, the saints, spiritual writers, and popes have all described the struggle between good and evil in military terms. Pope Francis often takes up this topic of our "spiritual battle" and gives it significant treatment in his 2018 Apostolic Exhortation "Gaudete et Exsultate" ("Rejoice and Be Glad").

The Battlefield Within Us

Evil is done in small things as in big things; in conflicts such as—for example—a boy or a girl who tells lies: it is a war against the truth of God, against the truth of life, against joy. This struggle between the devil and God, the Bible says will continue until the end. This is clear, isn't it? Do you understand this? It's clear. We all have a battlefield within us.

Address, Paul VI Audience Hall, Dec. 31, 2015

Fight of the Christian Life

Our heart, a saint once said, is like a "battlefield, a field of war where these two spirits struggle" and he called this a "spiritual battle." In the Christian life, one must fight to find space for the Spirit of God, and to cast away—like Jesus expelled the demon—the spirit of the world."

Meditation, Chapel of the
Domus Sanctae Marthae, Sept. 4, 2018

"Thorns of Satan"

We must prepare ourselves for the spiritual combat. This is important. It is impossible to preach the Gospel without this spiritual battle, a daily battle against sadness, against bitterness, against pessimism; a daily battle! Sowing is far from easy. Reaping is lovely but sowing is difficult and the daily battle of Christians consists in this.

Paul said he felt urgently impelled to preach and had had the experience of this spiritual fight, when he told us: "I have a thorn of Satan in my flesh and I feel it every day." We too have thorns of Satan that hurt us, that impede our progress and very often discourage us.

Address to Participants, Paul VI Audience Hall, June 17, 2013

Our Path to Holiness

God's word invites us clearly to "stand against the wiles of the devil" (Eph 6:11) and to "quench all the flaming darts of the evil one" (Eph 6:16). These expressions are not melodramatic, precisely because our path towards holiness is a constant battle. Those who do not realize this will be prey to failure or mediocrity.

Apostolic Exhortation, *Gaudete et Exsultate,*
(*On the Call to Holiness in Today's World*), no. 162

"Counterbalance to Evil"

Along this journey, the cultivation of all that is good, progress in the spiritual life and growth in love are the best counterbalance to evil. Those who choose to remain neutral, who are satisfied with little, who renounce the ideal of giving themselves generously to the Lord, will never hold out. Even less if they fall into defeatism, for "if we start without confidence, we have already lost half the battle and we bury our talents . . . Christian triumph is always a cross, yet a cross which is at the same time a victorious banner, borne with aggressive tenderness against the assaults of evil"(*Evangelii Gaudium*, no. 85).

Apostolic Exhortation, *Gaudete et Exsultate,*
(*On the Call to Holiness in Today's World*), no. 163

Discernment

Another frequent theme of Pope Francis is his emphasis on discernment of spirits. Amid all the mixed messages, trends, and attractions in our culture, we must be able to prayerfully distinguish good from evil, light from darkness, the voice of Christ from the enticement of the devil—keeping our eyes on eternity rather than upon the things of this world.

Christians "Must Know How to Discern"

How can I know whether something is of the Holy Spirit or of worldliness, whether of the spirit of the world or of the spirit of the devil? . . .

The instrument that the Spirit himself gives us is discernment: to discern, in any case, as one must do. This is what the Apostles did. They met, they spoke and they saw that this was the path of the Holy Spirit. . . . Those who did not have this gift, or who had not prayed, so as to ask for it, remained closed and still. . . .

[Christians] must know how to discern, especially at a time with so much communication, with so many novelties, to know how to discern: to discern one thing from another, to discern which is the novelty, the new wine that comes from God; which is news that comes from the spirit of the world and which is news that comes from spirit of the devil.

Meditation, Chapel of the
Domus Sanctae Marthae, May 8, 2017

Light and Darkness

We should ask the Lord insistently for the wisdom of discernment in order to recognize when it is Jesus who gives us light and when it is the devil himself, disguised as an angel of light. Many believe they live in light but they are in darkness and are unaware of it! If we are meek in our inner light, we are gentle people we hear the voice of Jesus in our heart and look fearlessly at the Cross in the light of Jesus. . . .

We must always make the distinction: where Jesus is there is always humility, meekness, love and the Cross. . . . Jesus didn't need an army to cast out demons, he didn't need pride or force or arrogance. . . .

Let us ask the Lord that he give us today the grace of his light and teach us to distinguish his light and the artificial light emitted by the enemy to deceive us.

Meditation, Chapel of the
Domus Sanctae Marthae, Sept. 3, 2013

Authentic Peace of Jesus

At work, in tasks, the challenge is to find that peace which means that the Lord accompanies you, that the Lord is close. And there is also another challenge: to know how to distinguish the peace of Jesus from another kind of peace which is not of Jesus. Do you understand? This is something that you must learn well, and ask the Lord for the grace to know how to discern true peace from false peace. To discern. This is a challenge. And true peace always comes from Jesus. Sometimes it comes "wrapped" in a cross. . . .

The challenge for all of us—mine too—is always to seek the peace of Jesus; even in dark times, but the peace of Jesus. And to know how to distinguish it from that other false kind of peace, which in the end is dishonest: it ends badly and does not reward you properly. Jesus is a good payer, he pays well: he pays very well!

Address, Eucharistic Youth Movement,
Paul VI Audience Hall, Aug. 7, 2015

Consider the Source

A Christian cannot be calm, assuming that everything is fine. He must discern things and really look at where they come from, what their root is . . . Where does this come from? What is the origin of this opinion, these phenomena?

Meditation, Chapel of the
Domus Sanctae Marthae, Oct. 9, 2015

The Lies of False Prophets

[E]ach of us is called to peer into our heart to see if we are falling prey to the lies of these false prophets. We must learn to look closely, beneath the surface, and to recognize what leaves a good and lasting mark on our hearts, because it comes from God and is truly for our benefit.

In his description of hell, Dante Alighieri pictures the devil seated on a throne of ice, in frozen and loveless isolation. We might well ask ourselves how it happens that charity can turn cold within us. What are the signs that indicate that our love is beginning to cool?

Message for Lent 2018

Gift of the Holy Spirit

May you, his children in our time, practice discernment to recognize what comes from the Holy Spirit and what comes from the spirit of the world or the spirit of the devil. Discernment "calls for something more than intelligence t is a gift which we must implore" of thout the wisdom of discernment, we rey to every passing trend" (Apostolic *et Exsultate*, nos. 166-167).

Address, Clementine Hall, April 19, 2018

ing"

f something comes from the Holy Spirit ne spirit of the world or the spirit of the is through discernment, which calls for an intelligence or common sense. It is a gift which we must implore. If we ask with confidence that the Holy Spirit grant us this gift, and then seek to develop it through prayer, reflection, reading and good counsel, then surely we will grow in this spiritual endowment.

The gift of discernment has become all the more necessary today, since contemporary life offers immense possibilities for action and distraction, and the world presents all of them as valid and good. All of us, but especially the young, are immersed in a culture of zapping. We can navigate simultaneously on two or more screens and interact at the same time with two or three virtual scenarios. Without the wisdom of discernment, we can easily become prey to every passing trend.

This is all the more important when some novelty presents itself in our lives. Then we have to decide whether it is new wine brought by God or an illusion created by the spirit of this world or the spirit of the devil. At other times, the opposite can happen, when the forces of evil induce us not to change, to leave things as they are, to opt for a rigid resistance to change. Yet that would be to block the working of the Spirit. We are free, with the freedom of Christ. Still, he asks us to examine what is within us—our desires, anxieties, fears and questions—and what takes place all around us—"the signs of the times"—and thus to recognize the paths that lead to complete freedom. "Test everything; hold fast to what is good" (1 Thes 5:21).

Apostolic Exhortation, *Gaudete et Exsultate*,
(*On the Call to Holiness in Today's World*), nos. 166-175

Examination of Conscience

An indispensable element of discernment is the regular examination of conscience. Pope Francis often calls for such examination and suggests questions to probe and guide our conscience in discernment.

"Did I Guard My Heart?"

We can ask ourselves: Do I keep watch over myself? Do I guard my heart? My feelings? My thoughts? Do I guard the treasure of grace? Do I protect the Holy Spirit's presence within me? If we do not protect this presence, one stronger than he assails him and overcomes him, he takes away his armor in which he trusted, and divides his spoil. . . .

Let us ask the Lord for the grace to take these things seriously. He came to battle for our salvation, and he has conquered the devil.

Meditation, Chapel of the
Domus Sanctae Marthae, Oct. 11, 2013

Bedtime Prayers

Which spirit did I follow today? The spirit of God or the spirit of the world? . . . This is to be done as a prayer, before going to bed, today, asking ourselves what kinds of feelings we had, identifying which spirit prompted us to which sentiments: the spirit of the world or the Spirit of God? . . .

If we are honest, we will often find that "today I was envious, I was greedy." . . . We all face this interior battle, but if we do not understand how these two spirits work, how they act, we will be unable to move forward with the Spirit of God which helps us to understand Christ's thoughts, the meaning of Christ. . . .

It is very simple. We have this great gift, which is the Spirit of God, but we are weak, we are sinners, and we also have the temptation of the spirit of the world. [And] in this spiritual battle, in this war of the spirit, we must be victors like Jesus, but we must know the path to take. [This is why] an examination of conscience is so useful, to look back on the day in the evening and say, "Yes, I was tempted in this way today, I was victorious here, the Holy Spirit inspired me." . . .

If we do not do this, if we do not know what happens in our heart--and I don't say this, the Bible does--we are like "animals that understand nothing," that move along through instinct. [But] we are not animals, we are children of God, baptized with the gift of the Holy Spirit . . . This is why it is important to understand what happened in my heart today. May the Lord teach us to make an examination of conscience every day.

Meditation, Chapel of the
Domus Sanctae Marthae, Sept. 4, 2018

Hidden Idols

Today there are many idols and many idolaters . . . We all have an idol hidden within us. We might ask ourselves before God: "What is my hidden idol, what occupies the Lord's place in my heart?"

Meditation, Chapel of the
Domus Sanctae Marthae, Oct. 15, 2013

Worship God or the Devil?

The devil began to test [Jesus] at the beginning of his time in the desert. And he sought to convince him to take another, more reasonable, more serene and less dangerous path. At last, the devil revealed his intention: if you worship me I will give you this! He sought to be his god. . . .

Do I worship God? Do I adore Jesus Christ the Lord? Or do I do so by halves and play games with the prince of this world? Worshipping to the very end with trust and fidelity is the grace we should ask.

Meditation, Chapel of the
Domus Sanctae Marthae, Nov. 28, 2013

Are We Free Children or Slaves?

Contemporaneously, the very gift for which we give thanks is also a reason for an examination of conscience, for a revision of our personal and communal life, to ask ourselves: what is our lifestyle? Do we live as children or as slaves? Do we live as people baptized in Christ, anointed by the Spirit, delivered and free? Or do we live according to the corrupt, worldly logic, doing what the devil makes us believe is in our interests?

Homily, Vatican Basilica, Dec. 31, 2014

Use of the Tongue

It will do us good to ask ourselves: Do I sow peace? For example, with my tongue, do I sow peace or do I sow discord? . . . How many times have we heard that a person has a serpent's tongue, because he does what the serpent did with Adam and Eve, he destroyed the peace?

Meditation, Chapel of the
Domus Sanctae Marthae, Sept. 4, 2015

Did I Let the Demon In?

Vigilance is necessary, because the enemy may come. . . . The Church advises us to always use an examination of conscience: What happened in my heart today, and why? Did this well-mannered demon and his friends try to come to my house?

Meditation, Chapel of the
Domus Sanctae Marthae, Oct. 9, 2015

Faith and Trust

To combat the devil's temptations, our faith must be strong. We must place our trust in God and look to the Cross of Christ for this strength.

Forward with Faith

One thing that would really help us would be to ask ourselves: "How is my faith? Do I believe or not? Or do I partly believe and partly not? Am I somewhat worldly and somewhat a believer?" . . .

[Are we aware that] without faith we can't go forward, we can't safeguard the salvation of God? . . . [I]f our faith is weak, the Devil will defeat us.

Meditation, Chapel of the
Domus Sanctae Marthae, Oct. 30, 2014

"God Is Stronger"

I would like to say out loud: God is stronger! Do you believe this, that God is stronger? Let us say it together, let us say it all together: God is stronger! And do you know why he is stronger? Because He is Lord, the only Lord. And I would like to add that reality, at times dark and marked by evil, can change, if we first bring the light of the Gospel especially through our lives.

General Audience, St. Peter's Square, June 12, 2013

God Is Our Hope

The second reading of the Mass presents a dramatic scene: a woman—an image of Mary and the Church—is being pursued by a Dragon—the devil—who wants to devour her child. But the scene is not one of death but of life, because God intervenes and saves the child (cf Rev 12:13a, 15-16a).

How many difficulties are present in the life of every individual, among our people, in our communities; yet as great as these may seem, God never allows us to be overwhelmed by them. In the face of those moments of discouragement we experience in life, in our efforts to evangelize or to embody our faith as parents within the family, I would like to say forcefully: Always know in your heart that God is by your side; he never abandons you! Let us never lose hope! Let us never allow it to die in our hearts!

The "dragon," evil, is present in our history, but it does not have the upper hand. The one with the upper hand is God, and God is our hope!

Homily, World Youth Day, Basilica of the Shrine of Our Lady of the Conception of Aparecida, July 24, 2013

Trust in God Overcomes Fear of Commitment

[Regarding fear of making a commitment to marriage, a fear that sometimes comes "from the devil"]

Call out to God, extend your hearts to him and he will lift you in his arms and show you how to love. I ask young couples in particular to trust that God wants to bless their love and their lives with his grace in the sacrament of marriage. God's gift of love is at the heart of Christian marriage, not the costly parties which often obscure the deep spiritual meaning of this day of joyful celebration with family and friends.

Address, Kololo Air Strip, Kampala, Uganda, Nov. 28, 2015

Jesus

[T]he only One who casts out demons is Jesus. The only One who heals these matters is Jesus. For this reason I say to each one of you: let yourself be healed by Jesus.

Homily, "San Michele Arcangelo a Pietralata" Parish, Rome, Italy, Feb. 8, 2015

Jesus Protects Us

This is the vocation and the joy of every baptized person: to reveal and give Jesus to others; but in order to do this we must know him and bear him within us, as the Lord of our life.

He protects us from the evil one, from the devil, who is always lurking at our door, at our heart, and wants to get in.

Angelus, St. Peter's Square, Jan. 3, 2016

Christ, Our Servant King

[Reflecting on the crucifixion account in Luke's Gospel]

They provoke him in the same way: "Save yourself!" (Lk 23:35, 37, 39). This temptation is worse than that of the people. . . . When confronted with this attack on his very way of being, Jesus does not speak, he does not react. He does not defend himself, he does not try to convince them, he does not mount a defense of his kingship. He continues rather to love; he forgives, he lives this moment of trial according to the Father's will, certain that love will bear fruit.

Homily, Solemnity of Christ, King of the Universe,
St. Peter's Square, Nov. 20, 2016

Look to the Cross of Christ

Jesus was lifted up and Satan was destroyed. We must be attracted to the cross of Jesus: we must look at it because it gives us the strength to go forward. And the ancient serpent that was destroyed still barks, still threatens but, as the Fathers of the Church say, he is a chained dog: do not approach him and he will not bite you; but if you try to caress him because you attracted to him as if he were a puppy, prepare yourself, he will destroy you."

The cross teaches us that in life there is failure and victory. We must be capable of tolerating defeat, of bearing our failures patiently, even those of our sins because He paid for us. We must tolerate them in Him, asking forgiveness in Him, but never allowing ourselves to be seduced by this chained dog.

It will be good if today, when we go home, we would take 5, 10, 15 minutes in front of the crucifix, either the one we have in our house or on the rosary: look at it, it is our sign of defeat, it provokes persecutions, it destroys us; it is also our sign of victory because it is where God was victorious.

Meditation, Chapel of the
Domus Sanctae Marthae, Sept. 14, 2018

Eyes on Christ

In order to receive the kingship of Jesus, we are called to struggle against this temptation, called to fix our gaze on the Crucified One, to become ever more faithful to him.

How many times, even among ourselves, do we seek out the comforts and certainties offered by the world? How many times are we tempted to come down from the Cross?

The lure of power and success seem an easy, quick way to spread the Gospel; we soon forget how the Kingdom of God works.

Homily, Solemnity of Christ, King of the Universe,
St. Peter's Square , Nov. 20, 2016

Vigilance

As in the parable of the ten virgins awaiting the bridegroom, we must remain vigilant, Pope Francis reminds us. As we have seen, the devil never rests, and so we can never let down our guard. It's not merely a matter of being strong against our weak tendencies but a true battle against the devil himself. As Christ told his Apostles in the Garden of Gethsemane, "Watch and pray that you may not undergo the test. The spirit is willing, but the flesh is weak." (Mt 26:41). Or, as Peter writes in another passage Pope Francis cites, "Be sober and vigilant. Your opponent the devil is prowling around like a roaring lion looking for [someone] to devour" (1 Pt 5:8).

Keeping Our Lamps Lit

The path of holiness is a source of peace and joy, given to us by the Spirit. At the same time, it demands that we keep "our lamps lit" (Lk 12:35) and be attentive. "Abstain from every form of evil" (1 Thes 5.22). "Keep awake" (Mt 24:42; Mk 13:35). "Let us not fall asleep" (1 Thes 5:6). Those who think they commit no grievous sins against God's law can fall into a state of dull lethargy. Since they see nothing serious to reproach themselves with, they fail to realize that their spiritual life has gradually turned lukewarm. They end up weakened and corrupted.

Spiritual corruption is worse than the fall of a sinner, for it is a comfortable and self-satisfied form of blindness. Everything then appears acceptable: deception, slander, egotism and other subtle forms of self-centeredness, for "even Satan disguises himself as an angel of light" (2 Cor 11:14).

Apostolic Exhortation, *Gaudete et Exsultate*,
(*On the Call to Holiness in Today's World*), nos. 164-165

Eternal Salvation Is at Stake

We cannot obtain the victory of Jesus over evil and the devil by halves, [for] "he who is not with me is against me, and he who does not gather with me scatters."

On this point, there is no shadow of a doubt. A battle exists, a battle in which the eternal salvation of us all is at stake. . . . We must always be vigilant against the deception and seduction of the evil one.

Meditation, Chapel of the
Domus Sanctae Marthae, Oct. 11, 2013

Holding Vigil Against Worldliness

[T]o hold vigil is to understand what enters my heart; it means to stop and examine my life. . . . Am I a Christian? Am I raising my children well? Is my life Christian or is it worldly? How might I understand this? . . .

Do I look to the crucified Christ? Do I at times, walk the Via Crucis in order to see the price of salvation, the price that has saved us not only from sin but also from worldliness?

Meditation, Chapel of the
Domus Sanctae Marthae, Oct. 13, 2017

Sentry at the Door

Am I the sentry of my heart? . . . Who among us, when we are at home, whether in the kitchen, or at our desk, wherever we may be, and seeing a person pass through that we don't know, who among us remains calm? No one! . . . "Who are you? Who let you in? Where did you come in?"

How many times do wicked thoughts enter, wicked intentions, jealousy, envy? So many things that enter. But who opened that door? Where did they come in?

Meditation, Chapel of the
Domus Sanctae Marthae, Oct. 10, 2014

Struggle Against More Than Our Weakness

We are not dealing merely with a battle against the world and a worldly mentality that would deceive us and leave us dull and mediocre, lacking in enthusiasm and joy. Nor can this battle be reduced to the struggle against our human weaknesses and proclivities (be they laziness, lust, envy, jealousy or any others). It is also a constant struggle against the devil, the prince of evil. Jesus himself celebrates our victories. He rejoiced when his disciples made progress in preaching the Gospel and overcoming the opposition of the evil one: "I saw Satan fall like lightning from heaven" (Lk 10:18).

Apostolic Exhortation, *Gaudete et Exsultate*,
(*On the Call to Holiness in Today's World*), no. 159

No Dialogue with Satan

A lesson to be drawn from Jesus' temptation in the wilderness is this: we must not engage the devil in dialogue. Eve, notes Pope Francis, held conversation with the serpent and was drawn into his deceit, whereas Jesus only responded to the devil's temptations by citing Scripture. "Only the power of God's Word will overcome [the devil]," the pope says.

Refuge in the Word

Jesus decisively rejects all these temptations and reiterates his firm resolve to follow the path set by the Father, without any kind of compromise with sin or worldly logic. Note well how Jesus responds. He does not dialogue with Satan, as Eve had done in the earthly paradise. Jesus is well aware that there can be no dialogue with Satan, for he is cunning. That is why Jesus, instead of engaging in dialogue as Eve had, chooses to take refuge in the Word of God and responds with the power of this Word.

Let us remember this: at the moment of temptation, of our temptations, there is no arguing with Satan, our defense must always be the Word of God! And this will save us. In his replies to Satan, the Lord, using the Word of God, reminds us above all that "man shall not live by bread alone, but by every word that proceeds from the mouth of God" (Mt 4:4;

cf. Dt 8:3); and this gives us the strength, sustains us in the struggle against a worldly mind-set that would lower man to the level of his primitive needs, causing him to lose hunger for what is true, good and beautiful, the hunger for God and for his love. Furthermore, he recalls that "it is written, 'You shall not tempt the Lord your God'" (Mt 4:7), for the way of faith passes also through darkness and doubt, and is nourished by patience and persevering expectation. Lastly, Jesus recalls that "it is written, 'You shall worship the Lord your God and him only you shall serve'" (Mt 4:10); i.e., we must rid ourselves of idols, of vain things, and build our lives on what is essential.

Jesus' words will then be borne out in his actions. His absolute fidelity to the Father's plan of love will lead him after about three years to the final reckoning with the "prince of this world" (Jn 16:11), at the hour of his Passion and Cross, and Jesus will have his final victory, the victory of love!

Angelus, St. Peter's Square , March 9, 2014

Don't Be Naïve or Foolish

The dialogue with Eve does not end well for Eve: Satan wins.

When the devil fools a person, he does so with dialogue; he seeks to dialogue. …

Jesus' three responses to the devil are taken from the Bible, from the Old Testament, from the Word of God, because one cannot dialogue with the devil.

Today the Church, with this Liturgy of the Word, teaches us not to be naïve, not to be foolish, to have our eyes open and to ask the Lord for help. . . . In temptation you do not dialogue, you pray: "Help, Lord, I am weak; I do not want to hide from you." . . . [W]hen you begin to dialogue you will end up beaten, defeated.

Meditation, Chapel of the
Domus Sanctae Marthae, Feb. 10, 2017

Not with That "Prince"

You cannot dialogue with the prince of the world. . . . With that prince, there is no dialogue; you can only answer him with the Word of God who defends us.

Meditation, Chapel of the
Domus Sanctae Marthae, May 4, 2013

"I Will Not Speak to You"

If we take the account of the temptation of Jesus, we never find his own words. Jesus does not answer with his own words; he answers in the words of Scripture, all three times. This is what he teaches us. One cannot dialogue with the devil, and this helps so much when temptation comes: I will not speak to you; only through the Word of the Lord.

Homily, Chapel of the Governorate, Oct. 3, 2015

Only the Words of God

We have chosen Jesus, not the evil one. If we remember what we heard in the Gospel, Jesus does not reply to the devil with any of his own words, but rather he the words of God, the words of Scripture. Because brothers and sisters, and let us be clear about this, we cannot dialogue with the devil, we cannot do this because he will always win. Only the power of God's word can overcome him.

Homily, Area of the Study Center of Ecatepec, Feb. 14, 2016

Patience, Astuteness, and Joy

The devil is patient and cunning, but we can be patient and cunning in response. Through prudence or astuteness we practice vigilance; if we live by the Gospel, we can maintain joy and even rejoice in the good of others, an attitude that will "banish the devil," says Pope Francis. Satan tries to wear us down so that we might give up the spiritual battle, but we must remain strong and exercise greater patience than he.

Do Not Worry

Let us ask the Lord to always say to us, in times of temptation, as he did with the disciples, with patience: Stop. Do not worry. Lift up your eyes, look to the horizon. Do not close yourself in, move forward. His Word will save us from falling into sin in moments of temptation.

Meditation, Chapel of the
Domus Sanctae Marthae, Feb. 18, 2014

"Unshakeable Trust"

There must be no confusion between good and evil! In the face of weeds present in the world, the disciple of the Lord is called to imitate God's patience, to foster hope with the support of an unshakeable trust in the final victory of the good, meaning God.

Our Father: Reflections on the Lord's Prayer (Image, 2018), p. 108

Avoid Temptation

Or here's another image: the devil is like a dog that is tied up and barks and growls. But if you don't get close to him, he can't bite you.

"Dear Pope Francis: The Pope Answers Letters from Children Around the World," Loyola Press (2016), p. 23

Move Forward in Crisis

When one faces a crisis—like when Jesus told Peter that the devil would put him in crisis ["sift"] as is done with wheat, and many times the devil, life, a neighbor, many people make us "jump" like the wheat, they put us in crisis—there is always a danger, a risk, risk in a bad sense, and an opportunity.

A Christian—this I have learned—should not be afraid to face a crisis: it is a sign that he is moving forward, that he is not anchored to the shore of a river or the sea, that he has set sail and is moving forward. And there are problems, crises, inconsistencies, and the crisis of one's own sin, which make us so ashamed. How does one avoid growing weary? It is a grace. Ask it of the Lord: "Lord, let me not grow weary. Give me the grace of patience, to move forward, to wait for peace to come."

Address, Visit to Villa Nazareth, Rome, Italy, June 18, 2016

Keep Doing Good in Spite of "Weariness of Enemies"

There is also the kind of weariness which we can call "the weariness of enemies." The devil and his minions never sleep and, since their ears cannot bear to hear the word of God, they work tirelessly to silence that word and to distort it.

Confronting them is more wearying. It involves not only doing good, with all the exertion this entails, but also defending the flock and oneself from evil (cf. *Evangelii Gaudium*, 83). The evil one is far more astute than we are, and he is able to demolish in a moment what it took us years of patience to build up.

Homily, Chrism Mass, Vatican Basilica, April 2, 2015

Guard Faith Through the Virtue of Cunning

One aspect of the light which guides us on the journey of faith is holy "cunning." This holy "cunning" is also a virtue. It consists of a spiritual shrewdness which enables us to recognize danger and avoid it. The Magi used this light of "cunning" when, on the way back, they decided not to pass by the gloomy palace of Herod, but to take another route These wise men from the East teach us how not to fall into the snares of darkness and how to defend ourselves from the shadows which seek to envelop our life. By this holy "cunning," the Magi guarded the faith.

We too need to guard the faith, guard it from darkness. Many times, however, it is a darkness under the guise of light. This is because the devil, as St. Paul, says, disguises himself at times as an angel of light. And this is where a holy "cunning" is necessary in order to protect the faith, guarding it from those alarmist voices that exclaim: "Listen, today we must do this, or that . . ."

Faith though, is a grace, it is a gift. We are entrusted with the task of guarding it, by means of this holy "cunning" and by prayer, love, charity. We need to welcome the light of God into our hearts and, at the same time, to cultivate that spiritual cunning which is able to combine simplicity with astuteness, as Jesus told his disciples: "Be wise as serpents and innocent as doves" (Mt 10:16)

Homily, Solemnity of the Epiphany of the Lord,
Vatican Basilica, Jan. 6, 2014

Seek Gospel Joy

We are called to respond to this worldly astuteness with Christian astuteness, which is a gift of the Holy Spirit. This is a matter of departing from the worldly spirit and values, which the devil really favors, in order to live according to the Gospel. How is worldliness manifested? Worldliness is manifested by attitudes of corruption, deception, subjugation, and it constitutes the most ill-chosen road, the road of sin, because one leads you to the other! It's like a chain, even if—it's true—it is generally the easiest road to travel.

Instead, the spirit of the Gospel requires a serious lifestyle—serious but joyful, full of joy!—serious and challenging, marked by honesty, fairness, respect for others and their dignity, and a sense of duty. And this is Christian astuteness!

Angelus, St. Peter's Square, Sept. 18, 2016

Rejoice for Others

It is not good when we look down on others like heartless judges, lording it over them and always trying to teach them lessons. That is itself a subtle form of violence. St. John of the Cross proposed a different path: "Always prefer to be taught by all, rather than to desire teaching even the least of all." And he added advice on how to keep the devil at bay: "Rejoice in the good of others as if it were your own, and desire that they be given precedence over you in all things; this you should do wholeheartedly. You will thereby overcome evil with good, banish the devil, and possess a happy heart. Try to practice this all the more with those who least attract you. Realize that if you do not train yourself in this way, you will not attain real charity or make any progress in it."

Apostolic Exhortation, *Gaudete et Exsultate*, (*On the Call to Holiness in Today's World*), no. 117

Curbing the Tongue

Pope Francis warns of how the devil works through gossip, slander, obscenity, and hypocrisy. As we've seen, he has even compared gossip to terrorism! He also suggests ways to avoid giving into these sins and thereby avoid doing the devil's divisive work for him.

Bite Your Tongue

Every time your mouth is about to say something that sows discord and divisiveness and to speak ill of another person, [just] bite your tongue! I assure you that if you do this exercise of biting your tongue instead of sowing discord, the first few times your tongue will swell, wounded, because the devil helps to do this because it is his work, it is his job to divide!

Meditation, Chapel of the
Domus Sanctae Marthae, Sept. 4, 2015

Gossip Divides

The devil is a liar and, what is more, he is a gossip, he loves going from one place to the other, seeking to divide, and he wants members of a community to speak badly of each other. . . . The terrorist just like the devil goes in whispering and murmuring, throws the bomb, destroys and calmly walks off . . . You know the best remedy against gossip? Bite your tongue. The infirmary sister will have a lot of work because there will be swollen tongues but at least bombs will not be thrown.

Homily, Midday Prayer, Shrine of the Lord of the Miracles, Lima, Peru, Jan. 21, 2018

Pray, Then Speak Calmly

If you have something against your brother, against your sister, go. . . . First pray, calm your soul, and then go and say to him, to her: "I do not agree with this . . . you have done a bad thing . . ." However, never, never drop the bomb of gossip. Never, ever!

Address, Paul VI Audience Hall, Sept. 17, 2015

Stop the "Trickle of Water"

[This] is the way gossip works, and we have all been tempted to gossip. . . . I too have been tempted to gossip! It is a daily temptation [that] begins slowly, like a trickle of water. . . .

[We must] be careful when we feel something in our heart that would lead to destroying people, destroying reputations, destroying our lives, leading us into worldliness and sin. . . . [I]f we do not stop ourselves in time, that trickle of water, when it grows and spreads, will become a tidal wave that leads us to justify ourselves.

Meditation, Chapel of the
Domus Sanctae Marthae, April 11, 2014

Being with the Lord

A community, a family is destroyed by this envy that the devil teaches in the heart and causes one to speak ill of the other. . . .

[T]hat there may be peace in a community, in a family, in a country, in the world, we must start by being with the Lord. And where the Lord is there is no envy, there is no crime, there is no jealousy; there is brotherhood.

Let us ask this of the Lord: never to kill our neighbor with our tongue, and to be with the Lord just as we shall all be in heaven.

Meditation, Chapel of the
Domus Sanctae Marthae, Sept. 2, 2013

Children of Light or of Darkness?

[Reflecting on the Letter to the Ephesians (4:32-5:8)]

St. Paul says to the Christians that we must behave as children of light and not as children of darkness, as we once were. . . . [T]o explain this, both he and the Gospel (Lk 13:10-17) offer a catechesis on language: what is the speech of a child of light and what is the speech of a child of darkness?

Today the Church leads us to reflect on the way of speaking, and from this she will help us to understand whether we are children of light or children of darkness. . . .

Remember: no obscene language! No vulgar and worldly words! No vacuous words! No hypocritical words! [These types of speech] do not belong to God, they belong to the Evil One. . . .

How do we speak? Which of these four [types of] words do we speak with? Obscene words, worldly, vulgar words, vacuous words, hypocritical words? . . . Am I a Christian of light? Am I a Christian of darkness? Am I a Christian of grayness?

Meditation, Chapel of the
Domus Sanctae Marthae, Oct. 27, 2014

Hypocrisy, the Devil's Language

[Hypocrisy uses] the same language as the devil who sows that duplicitous language in communities in order to destroy them. [Therefore,] let us ask the Lord to protect us from falling into this vice of hypocrisy, [from] masking our attitude, but with evil intentions. That the Lord might give us this grace: "Lord, that I might never be a hypocrite, that I might know how to speak the truth and if I cannot say it, to stay silent, but never hypocrisy."

Meditation, Chapel of the
Domus Sanctae Marthae, June 6, 2017

Forgiveness and Service

Jesus came to bring God's mercy to a world in the grip of evil; in imitating Christ, we show mercy by forgiving and serving others. The devil's hatred and worldliness cannot coexist with mercy.

Forgive Those Who Hate and Persecute

Jesus did not say: "Poor you if these things happen to you!" No, he said: "Blessed are you when men revile you and persecute you and utter all kinds of evil against you falsely on my account. Rejoice and be glad."

The devil cannot abide the Church's holiness. . . . He stirred up hatred in the hearts of those people against Stephen, to persecute him, to revile him, and to utter all kinds of evil against him. . . . [But Stephen] died like Jesus, forgiving, [repeating] the very words of Jesus: “Lord, do not hold this sin against them.”

Meditation, Chapel of the Domus Sanctae Marthae, May 6, 2014

Like the Saints, Overcome Hate with Service

This is the life of a Saint. Saints are people who for love of God did not put conditions on him in their life; they were not hypocrites; they spent their lives at the service of others. They suffered much adversity but without hate.

The Saints never hated. Understand this well: love is of God, then from whom does hatred come? Hatred does not come from God but from the devil! And the Saints removed themselves from the devil; the Saints are men and women who have joy in their hearts and they spread it to others. Never hate but serve others, the most needy; pray and live in joy. This is the way of holiness!

Angelus, Solemnity of All Saints, St. Peter’s Square, Nov. 1, 2013

Acts of Charity

It would do us well to fracture, not one's bones, but to fracture one's convenient attitudes [through] acts of charity. . . . "I am comfortable, but I will do that which costs me"—[for example,] visit a sick person, give help to someone in need: an act of charity. This, according to [Saint] Francis, breaks down the spiritual worldliness in the person that the demons seek to create. . . .

Acts of charity, those that are costly, will lead us to be more attentive and more vigilant, such that these sly characters cannot enter.

Meditation, Chapel of the
Domus Sanctae Marthae, Oct. 13, 2017

Friendship, Community, Solidarity

We are called to communion. Jesus prayed that his faithful "may all be one" (Jn 17:21), united in faith. Unity protects us from the divisions the devil wants to create among us.

Recognizing God's Image

In a Christian community, division is one of the gravest sins, because it makes it a sign not of God's work, but of the devil's work, who is by definition the one who separates, who destroys relationships, who insinuates prejudice. . . .

Division in a Christian community, whether in a school, a parish, or an association, it is a very grave sin, because it is the work of the Devil. God, instead wants us to develop the capacity to welcome, to forgive and to love each other, to be ever more like Him, who is communion and love.

The Church's holiness consists in this: in recognizing herself in God's image, showered with his mercy and his grace.

General Audience, St. Peter's Square, Aug. 27, 2014

The Unity of the Trinity

Seek unity in the renewal, because unity comes from the Holy Spirit and is born of the unity of the Trinity. Who is the source of division? The devil! Division comes from the devil. Flee from all infighting, please! Let there be none of this among you!

Address, Olympic Stadium, June 1, 2014

Friendship and Fraternity

What did the Lord say? When the devil sows weeds, let them grow. You grow good grain, friendship. And at harvest time the weeds will be burned and the good grain will bear its fruit.

I ask you to always maintain a climate of friendship and fraternity in which to pray and to share on a weekly basis experiences, apostolic successes and failures.

Address to Participants, Paul VI Audience Hall, April 30, 2015

Seek Solidarity

Perhaps the most powerful message that you can offer to those around you is this faith that reaches out in solidarity. The devil wants you to quarrel among yourselves, because in this way he divides you, he defeats you, and he robs you of faith. Therefore, solidarity among brothers and sisters to defend the faith!

Address, Chapel of San Juan Bautista,
Asunción, Paraguay, July 12, 2015

Maintain Marital Unity

I offer this advice to spouses: argue as much as you want, but don't let the day end without making peace. Do you know why? Because "the cold war" of the day after is extremely dangerous. How many marriages are saved when they have the courage at the end of the day to not make speeches but rather offer a caress, and peace is made!

It is true, there are more complex situations, when the devil gets involved and entices the man with another woman who seems more beautiful than his wife, or when the devil entices the woman with another man who seems better than her husband. Ask for help straightaway. When this temptation comes, ask for help immediately.

Address, Church of the Assumption of the Blessed Virgin Mary, Tbilisi, Georgia (Europe), Oct. 1, 2016

Avoid Isolation

When we live apart from others, it is very difficult to fight against concupiscence, the snares and temptations of the devil and the selfishness of the world. Bombarded as we are by so many enticements, we can grow too isolated, lose our sense of reality and inner clarity, and easily succumb.

Growth in holiness is a journey in community, side by side with others.

Apostolic Exhortation, *Gaudete et Exsultate*, (*On the Call to Holiness in Today's World*), nos. 140-141

Unity Despite Differences

Please, fight against division, because it is one of the weapons that the devil uses to destroy the local Church and the universal Church. In particular the differences, owing to the various ethnic groups present in the same territory, must not penetrate the Christian communities to the point of prevailing over their good. There are challenges that are difficult to resolve, but with the grace of God, prayer and penance, it can be done.

Address, Clementine Hall, Sept. 9, 2016

Scripture and the Commandments

As Christ demonstrated in the wilderness, the Word of God can turn Satan away. Scripture provides us with strength for our battle against the devil. And if we focus on doing God's will and not listening to the Evil One, we will keep and freely embrace the commandments.

Learn from the Gospels

The devil exists even in the 21st century. And we must not be naive. We must Learn from the Gospel how to battle against him.

Meditation, Chapel of the
Domus Sanctae Marthae, April 11, 2014

Treat the Bible Like Our Cell Phone?

During the 40 days of Lent, as Christians we are invited to follow in Jesus' footsteps and face the spiritual battle with the Evil One with the strength of the Word of God. Not with our words: they are worthless. The Word of God: this has the strength to defeat Satan. For this reason, it is important to be familiar with the Bible: read it often, meditate on it, assimilate it. The Bible contains the Word of God, which is always timely and effective.

Someone has asked: What would happen were we to treat the Bible as we treat our mobile phone? Were we to always carry it with us, or at least a small, pocket-sized Gospel, what would happen? Were we to turn back when we forget it: you forget your mobile phone—"Oh! I don't have it, I'm going back to look for it"? Were we to open it several times a day, were we to read God's messages contained in the Bible as we read telephone messages, what would happen? Clearly the comparison is paradoxical, but it calls for reflection.

Indeed, if we had God's Word always in our heart, no temptation could separate us from God, and no obstacle could divert us from the path of good; we would know how to defeat the daily temptations of the evil that is within us and outside us; we would be more capable of living a life renewed according to the Spirit, welcoming and loving our brothers and sisters, especially the weakest and neediest, and also our enemies.

Angelus, St. Peter's Square, March 5, 2017

Lectio Divina

There is one particular way of listening to what the Lord wishes to tell us in his word and of letting ourselves be transformed by the Spirit. It is what we call *lectio divina*. It consists of reading God's word in a moment of prayer and allowing it to enlighten and renew us. This prayerful reading of the

Bible is not something separate from the study undertaken by the preacher to ascertain the central message of the text; on the contrary, it should begin with that study and then go on to discern how that same message speaks to his own life. The spiritual reading of a text must start with its literal sense. Otherwise we can easily make the text say what we think is convenient, useful for confirming us in our previous decisions, suited to our own patterns of thought. Ultimately this would be tantamount to using something sacred for our own benefit and then passing on this confusion to God's people. We must never forget that sometimes "even Satan disguises himself as an angel of light" (2 Cor 11:14).

Apostolic Exhortation, *Evangelii Gaudium* (*The Joy of the Gospel*), no. 152

Commandments

We see what happened in the beginning. The Tempter, the devil, wants to deceive man and woman on this point: he wants to convince them that God has forbidden them to eat the fruit of the tree of [the knowledge of] good and evil in order to keep them submissive.

This is precisely the challenge: is the first rule that God gave to man a despot's imposition which forbids and compels, or is it the care of a father who is looking after his little ones and protecting them from self-destruction? Is it a word or a command? The most tragic among the various lies that the serpent tells Eve is the insinuation of an envious divinity—"But no, God envies you"—of a possessive divinity—"God does not want you to be free." The facts show dramatically that the serpent has lied (cf. Gn 2:16-17; 3:4-5); he made believe that a loving word was a command.

Man is at this crossroads: does God impose things on me or does he take care of me? Are his commandments merely a law or do they contain a word, to nurture me? Is God master or Father? God is Father: never forget this. Even in the worst situations, remember that we have a Father who loves us all.

Are we subjects or children? This battle, inside and outside of us, is constantly present: 1,000 times we have to choose between a slavish mentality and a mentality of children. A commandment is from the master; a word is from the Father. . . . The Commandments are the journey toward freedom. They set us free because they are the Word of the Father on this journey.

Angelus, St. Peter's Square, June 20, 2018

Prayer, Liturgy, Sacraments

"The 'spiritual battle' of the Christian's new life is inseparable from the battle of prayer," says the Catechism of the Catholic Church *(no. 2725). Pope Francis reminds us that we have many resources at our disposal for mounting our defense against the prince*

of this world, among these, prayer, the Mass, the sacraments, and the intercession of the Blessed Virgin Mary, our Mother.

"Powerful Weapons"

For this spiritual combat, we can count on the powerful weapons that the Lord has given us: faith-filled prayer, meditation on the word of God, the celebration of Mass, eucharistic adoration, sacramental reconciliation, works of charity, community life, missionary outreach. If we become careless, the false promises of evil will easily seduce us.

Apostolic Exhortation, *Gaudete et Exsultate,*
(*On the Call to Holiness in Today's World*), no. 162

Prayer, the Divine Office, the Mass

It is precisely in prayer, when the Spirit makes you feel something, the devil comes and makes you feel another; but prayer is the condition for moving forward. Even if prayer can often seem boring. Prayer is so important. Not only the prayer of the Divine Office, but the liturgy of the Mass, quiet, celebrated well with devotion, personal prayer with the Lord.

Address, Palatine Chapel in the
Royal Palace of Caserta, Caserta, Italy, July 26, 2014

Mother Mary, Our Refuge

Monks of old recommended, in times of trial, that we take refuge beneath the mantle of the Holy Mother of God: calling upon her as "Holy Mother of God" was already a guarantee of protection and help, this prayer over and again: "Holy Mother of God," "Holy Mother of God" . . . Just like this.

This wisdom, that comes to us from far off, helps us: the Mother protects the faith, safeguards relationships, saves those in storms and preserves them from evil. Where our Mother is at home, the devil does not enter in. Where our Mother is at home, the devil does not enter in. Where our Mother is present, turmoil does not prevail, fear does not conquer.

Homily, Basilica of St. Mary Major, Jan. 28, 2018

Mary and the Rosary

And in the struggle which the disciples must confront—all of us, all the disciples of Jesus, we must face this struggle—Mary does not leave them alone. the Mother of Christ and of the Church is always with us. She walks with us always, she is with us. And in a way, Mary shares this dual condition. She has of course already entered, once and for all, into heavenly glory. But this does not mean that she is distant or detached from us; rather Mary accompanies us, struggles with us, sustains Christians in their fight against the forces of evil. . . . [P]rayer with Mary, especially the rosary . . . has this "suffering" dimension, that is of struggle, a sustaining prayer in the battle against the evil one and his accomplices.

Homily, Feast of the Assumption,
Castel Gandolfo, Aug. 15, 2013

The Angels

On the journey and in the trials of life we are not alone, we are accompanied and sustained by the Angels of God, who offer, so to speak, their wings to help us overcome the many dangers, to be able to fly above those realities that can make our lives difficult or drag us down. In consecrating the Vatican City State to St. Michael the Archangel, let us ask him to defend us from the Evil One and cast him out.

Address, Blessing of the New Statue of St. Michael the Archangel, Vatican Gardens, July 5, 2013

Prayer and the Sacraments

Let us prepare ourselves for the spiritual combat: evangelization asks true courage of us partly because this inner fight, this battle in our hearts, so speak with prayer, with mortification, with the desire to follow Jesus, with the sacraments that are an encounter with Jesus, that are speaking to Jesus: thank you, thank you for your grace.

Address, Paul VI Audience Hall, June 17, 2013

The Church Invites Us to Conversion

We have opted for Jesus and not for the devil; we want to follow in Jesus' footsteps, even though we know that this is not easy. We know what it means to be seduced by money, fame and power. For this reason, the Church gives us the gift of this Lenten season, invites us to conversion, offering but one certainty: he is waiting for us and wants to heal our hearts of all that tears us down. He is the God who has a name: Mercy.

Homily, Area of the Study Center of Ecatepec, Feb. 14, 2016

Baptismal Commitment

At Baptism, and every time we renew our baptismal commitment, we renounce Satan and profess our faith in God. Through the power of the sacramental grace communicated through the ministry of the Church we find strength for our spiritual battle.

"Yes" to God, "No" to the Devil

Once the water of the font has been blessed, the heart must be prepared to accept Baptism. This occurs with the renunciation of Satan and the Profession of Faith, two actions which are closely connected. In the same measure with which I say "no" to the suggestions of the devil—the one who divides—I am able to say "yes" to God who calls me to conform to him in thoughts and deeds. The devil divides. God always unites the community, mankind, into one single people. It is not possible to adhere to Christ by placing conditions. It is necessary to detach oneself from certain bonds in order to truly embrace others. One is either well with God or well with the devil.

For this reason, the renunciation and the act of faith go together. It is necessary to burn some bridges, leaving them behind, in order to undertake the new Way which is Christ.

The response to the questions—"Do you renounce Satan, all his works and all his empty promises?"—is made in first person singular: "I do." And the profession of faith is made in the same way: "I believe." I renounce and I believe: this is the foundation of Baptism.

General Audience, St. Peter's Square, May 2, 2018

Baptism Prepares Us

Baptism is not a magical formula but a gift of the Holy Spirit who enables those who receive him to "fight against the spirit of evil," believing that God has sent his son into the world to destroy the power of Satan and to transfer mankind from darkness into the Kingdom of infinite light (cf. *Rite of Baptism for Children*, no. 49).

We know from experience that Christian life is always subject to temptation, especially to the temptation to separate oneself from God, from his will, from communion with him, to fall again into the snares of worldly seductions. And Baptism prepares us. It gives us strength for this daily struggle, even for the battle against the devil who, as St. Peter says, tries to devour us, to destroy us like a lion.

In addition to prayer, there is also the anointing of the breast of catechumens with oil: "it strengthens the candidates with the power to renounce the devil and sin before they go to the font of life for rebirth" (*Blessing of Oils and Chrism*, Introduction no. 2). Due to the ability of oil to penetrate and benefit bodily tissues, combatants in ancient times would spread oil over their bodies to tone their muscles and to escape more easily from the grip of their adversary. In light of this symbolism, Christians in the early centuries adopted the use of anointing the bodies of Baptismal candidates with oil blessed by the bishop to show through this "sign of salvation" that the power of Christ the Savior strengthens us to fight against evil and defeat it" (*Rite of Baptism for Children*, n. 87).

It is tiring to fight against evil, to escape its deceit, to regain strength after an exhausting battle, but we must know that all of Christian life is a battle. We must also know, however, that we are not alone, that Mother Church prays so that her children, reborn in Baptism, do not succumb to the snares of the evil one but overcome them through the power of the Paschal Christ.

Fortified by the Risen Christ who defeated the prince of this world (cf. Jn 12:31), we too can repeat with the faith of St. Paul: "I can do all things in him who strengthens me" (Phil 4:13). We all can overcome, overcome anything, but with the strength that comes from Jesus.

General Audience, St. Peter's Square, April 25, 2018

Refrain from Evil and Cling to Good

The promises of Baptism have two aspects: rejecting evil and clinging to good.

Rejecting evil means saying "no" to temptation, to sin, to Satan. More concretely, it means saying "no" to a culture of death that manifests itself in escaping from reality towards a false happiness that is expressed in lies, deceit, injustice and in despising others. "No" to all this. The new life given to us in Baptism has the Spirit as its wellspring and rejects any behavior dominated by feelings of division and discord. This is why the Apostle Paul urges that "all bitterness and wrath and anger and clamor and slander be put away from your hearts, with all malice" (cf. v. 31). This is what Paul says. These six elements or vices which unsettle the joy of the Holy Spirit, poison the heart and lead to cursing God and our neighbors.

But, it is not enough to refrain from doing evil in order to be a good Christian. It is necessary to cling to good and to do good. And then St. Paul continues: "be kind to one another, tenderhearted, forgiving one another, as God in Christ forgave you" (v. 32). Often, we happen to hear someone say: "I do no harm to anyone." And they think they are saints. All right, but do you do good? How many people do no evil but, at the same time, do no good, and their life goes by in indifference, apathy and tepidness. This attitude is contrary to the Gospel and it also goes against the temperament of you young people, who are by nature dynamic, passionate and brave. Remember this—if you remember it we can repeat it together: "It is good to do no evil, but it is evil to do no good." . . .

Do not feel all is well when you refrain from doing evil. Everyone is guilty of not doing the good they could have done. It is not enough to refrain from hate. One must forgive. It is not enough to refrain from bearing grudges. One must pray for one's enemies. It is not enough not to refrain from causing division. We must bring peace where there is none. It is not enough to refrain from speaking ill of others. We must interrupt when we hear others speak badly about someone: stopping the gossip: this is doing good.

If we do not oppose evil, we feed it tacitly. It is necessary to intervene where evil spreads because evil spreads in the absence of audacious Christians who oppose it with good, walking in love (cf. 5:2), according to St. Paul's admonition.

Angelus, St. Peter's Square, Aug. 12, 2018

CONCLUSION

Prayer to St. Michael and Christ's Final Victory

On Sept. 29, 2018, the Feast of the Archangels, Pope Francis invited the world's faithful to pray the Rosary daily during the entire month of October "to join in communion and in penitence, as the people of God, in asking the Holy Mother of God and St. Michael Archangel to protect the Church from the devil, who always seeks to separate us from God and from each other," said a Vatican statement.

The pope's intention for this request was to ask the Blessed Mother to preserve the Church "from the attacks by the devil, the great accuser," the statement said, "and at the same time to make her more aware of the faults, the errors and the abuses committed in the present and in the past, and committed to combating without any hesitation, so that evil may not prevail."

In addition, the pope asked that the faithful pray at the end of the Rosary the ancient Marian prayer *Sub Tuum Praesidium* and conclude with the traditional "Prayer to St. Michael the Archangel," which specifically seeks protection against Satan:

St. Michael the Archangel,
defend us in battle.
Be our defense against the wickedness and snares of the Devil.
May God rebuke him, we humbly pray,
and do thou,
O Prince of the heavenly hosts,
by the power of God,
thrust into hell Satan,
and all the evil spirits,
who prowl about the world
seeking the ruin of souls. Amen.

It was not the first time Pope Francis recommended this prayer. On the same date in 2014, Pope Francis said the feast was an especially suitable day to "recite that old but beautiful prayer to Michael the Archangel, that he continue to fight to defend humanity's greatest mystery: that the Word became man, died and rose again."

St. Michael—one of three angels named in Scripture, is first mentioned in the Book of Daniel, where he is described as a "great prince" who comforts Daniel and strengthens the Jewish people during their exile in Babylon. In the Letter of St. Jude, he is said to have disputed with the devil over the body of Moses. But it is in Revelation that his reputation as the warrior against Satan is sealed:

"Then war broke out in heaven; Michael and his angels battled against the dragon. The dragon and its angels fought back, but they did not prevail and there was no longer any place for them in heaven. The huge dragon, the ancient serpent,* who is called the Devil and Satan, who deceived the whole world, was thrown down to earth, and its angels were thrown down with it" (Rev 12:7-9).

By the power of God, St. Michael and his angels thus defeated the rebellious angels and cast them from heaven. Based on this Scripture passage, in sacred art St. Michael is frequently depicted as standing over a vanquished Satan while brandishing a sword or spear. For centuries the Christian faithful have called upon St. Michael to protect them from the devil's influence.

The "Prayer to St. Michael" was originally composed in 1884 by Pope Leo XIII after he experienced an apparently terrifying vision of evil spirits. He soon directed that it be added to the prayers recited at the end of every low Mass. These so-called Leonine Prayers were suppressed in 1964 as part of the Church's liturgical reforms, but in more recent years a number of local bishops have reinstituted the "Prayer to St. Michael" prior to the dismissal of the Mass. It remains a popular prayer of personal piety as well.

Pope Francis has urged the faithful to seek protection from Satan through St. Michael on multiple occasions.

St. Michael the Archangel, Pray for Us

Pope Francis frequently reminds us of the powerful intercessor we have in St. Michael the Archangel in our spiritual combat with "the devil, and all his works, and all his empty promises."

Defend Us

Let us ask the help of St. Michael the Archangel to defend us from the snares of the devil.

Twitter, Pope Francis @Pontifex, 6:15 AM · Oct 29, 2015

Our Helper in the Battle

The Lord asked [St. Michael] to fight [the devil] for us who are on our life journey towards heaven; Michael helps us to fight against him and to not be seduced by this evil spirit which deceives us.

Meditation, Chapel of the
Domus Sanctae Marthae, Sept. 29, 2017

War in Heaven

The First Reading, taken from the Book of Revelation, begins with a strong word: "War broke out in Heaven." And then it explains how this war was. It is the final war, the last war, the war of the end. It is the war between the Angels of God commanded by St Michael against Satan, the ancient serpent, the devil. This is the final one and everything ends there, only the Lord's eternal peace remains with all his children who were faithful. However, throughout history this war has been waged every day, every day: it is waged in the heart of men and women, in the hearts of Christians and of non-Christians. . . . It is the war between good and evil, where we must choose what we want, good or evil. But the strategy of war, the methods of war of these two enemies are totally opposite.

In the initial prayer, in the Collect, we asked for the grace to be defended by the Archangel Michael against the "snares" of the demon, of the devil. And snares are one of the strategies of the devil. He is a sower of snares. A seed of life, a seed of unity never falls from his hands—snares, always snares: it is his method, to sow snares. Let us pray to the Lord to safeguard us from this. . . .

This is our struggle, and therefore today let us ask the Lord that, through the intercession of the Archangel Michael, we may be protected from the snares, the fascination, the seductions of this ancient serpent called Satan. . . .

Pray often so that, with the intercession of St. Michael the Archangel, the Lord may safeguard you from giving in to every temptation, from every temptation to corruption for money, for riches, from vanity and arrogance.

Homily, Chapel of the Governorate, Oct. 3, 2015

"In Him It Is God Who Acts"

Michael—which means: "Who is like God?"—is the champion of the primacy of God, of his transcendence and power. Michael fights to reestablish divine justice; he defends the People of God from their enemies and above all from the arch-enemy *par excellence*, the devil.

And St. Michael triumphs because in him it is God who acts. This sculpture reminds us therefore that evil is vanquished, the accuser is unmasked, his head is crushed, because salvation was fulfilled once and for all by the blood of Christ. Even if the devil is always trying to scratch the face of the Archangel and the face of man, God is stronger; his is the victory and his salvation is offered to every human being. . . .

In consecrating the Vatican City State to St. Michael the Archangel, let us ask him to defend us from the Evil One and cast him out.

Address, Blessing of the New Statue of St. Michael the Archangel, Vatican Gardens, July 5, 2013

"Deliver Us from Evil"

In his 2018 book Our Father: Reflections on the Lord's Prayer, *Pope Francis provides a concise summary of his fundamental teachings about Satan, his works, and how we must respond:*

There is evil. Evil is not something intangible that spreads like the fog of Milan. Evil is a person, Satan, who is very cunning. The Lord tells us that when Satan is driven out he goes away, but after a certain time, when one is distracted, perhaps after several years, he comes back worse than before. He does not stage a home invasion. No, Satan is very courteous; he knocks at the door, rings, and enters with his typical seductions and his companions.

In the end, this is the meaning of the verse "deliver us from evil." We must be sly, in the good sense of the word, be sharp, have the ability to discern the lies of Satan—with whom I am convinced there is no dialoguing. How did Jesus act with Satan? He drove him way, or, as he did in the desert, he used the Word of God. Not even Jesus ever began a dialogue with Satan, because if we start to dialogue with him we are lost. He is more intelligent than we humans are. He turns us upside down and makes our heads spin. In the end we must say, "Be gone, be gone!"

Our Father: Reflections on the Lord's Prayer, (Image, 2018), p. 102-103

Victory of the Cross

"Jesus was lifted up and Satan was destroyed," said Pope Francis in a 2018 meditation on the Feast of the Holy Cross. "We must be attracted to the cross of Jesus: we must look at it because it gives us the strength to go forward . . . [I]t is also our sign of victory because it is where God was victorious" (Meditation, Sept. 14, 2018)

In reflecting on the final petition of the Lord's Prayer, "deliver us from evil," the Catechism of the Catholic Church *says that "Christians pray to God with the Church to show forth the victory, already won by Christ, over the 'ruler of this world,' Satan, the angel personally opposed to God and to his plan of salvation" (no. 2864). No matter what temptation befalls us or what evil exists in the world, we know that the devil, whom Pope Francis calls "a loser," has already been defeated by Christ's victory on Calvary. In closing, then, we offer this prayer of hope and confidence in the triumph of the Cross written by Pope Francis.*

O Cross of Christ,
teach us that the rising of the sun
Is more powerful than the darkness of night.
O Cross of Christ,
teach us that the apparent victory of evil
vanishes before the empty tomb
and before the certainty of the Resurrection
and the love of God
which nothing can defeat, obscure, or weaken.
Amen.

Prayer after Stations of the Cross,
Coliseum, Rome, March 25, 2016